MIND THE WINDOWS

WITH JACK WILSON

MIND THE WINDOWS

TINO BEST

MY STORY

JB
JOHN BLAKE

Published by John Blake Publishing Ltd,
3 Bramber Court, 2 Bramber Road,
London W14 9PB, England

www.johnblakebooks.com

www.facebook.com/johnblakebooks
twitter.com/jblakebooks

This edition published in hardback in 2016

ISBN: 978 1 78606 034 1

British Library Cataloguing-in-Publication Data:

A catalogue record for this book is available from the British Library.

Design by www.envydesign.co.uk

Printed in Great Britain by CPI Group (UK) Ltd

1 3 5 7 9 10 8 6 4 2

From Tino Best

I'd like to dedicate this to the following people. Without you, there'd be no book:

To my grandmother and her five daughters – including my beloved mum – who have been there for me since the start. Thank you.

To Denton Hoyte. You've been like a father to me, the only father I have known. I trust you with my life.

And to everyone at Empire Cricket Club. Thank you for teaching me how to play the wonderful game of cricket. That includes Sharon. I'm sure I used to annoy the hell out of you by asking you to bowl balls at me at every game as a seven-year-old. Thank you for doing it.

From Jack Wilson

Tino – I could have asked for no one better to work with. It has been an honour to both hear, and tell, your story. Thank you for letting me into your life. I hope I have done you justice.

To my good friend Rob 'Willow' Wilson, you will never be forgotten. I just wish you were here now: in the nets, or on a 300-track, ready to face Tino without a thigh pad. Always in our thoughts. Rest in peace, mate.

CONTENTS

FOREWORD

I'm on the honours board at Lord's twice. The first time was for scoring 142 against South Africa in 2003. The second? Five wickets against the Aussies in 2009 in my last ever Test at the home of cricket. Phil Hughes, Simon Katich and Brad Haddin were among my scalps. My name's up there with a load of greats forever. Happy days!

That five for ninety two helped us win our first Ashes Test there for 75 years. We took that series 2-1 and I was handed the man-of-the-match award. With it, I became one of a handful of players to get on the honours board with both bat and ball. Don't get better than that, does it?

But it does – apparently! I read a piece once that had my top cricketing moments in. It said that the five-for wasn't even my biggest achievement at Lord's. Really? So what was?

Sledging Tino, of course!

The West Indies liked a word or two. That series, Dwayne Bravo had already been in my ear when I was batting. Clapping, clapping, clapping away he was: 'Come on Fidy, come on Fidy, come on Fidy. Get the big man out Fidy boy, come on Fidy.' It did my head in – so I took a pop back at him. I asked him where he'd be in three years, then told him he wouldn't be here. It got a few laughs did that.

But that was nothing on poor Tino. I know he liked a big shot and there's that vast media centre at Lord's, full of glass windows. It's the home of cricket and I was worried about it, you see. What would happened if Tino creamed one through those windows? All that money spent on such a magnificent building. It'd be a shame if it got damaged…

So I gave him some friendly advice from slip: 'Mind the windows, Tino.' It was the least I could do.

But Tino didn't care much about those windows. Where's his respect for Lord's and its property? Ashley Giles floated one up there for him and Tino's eyes lit up. Those poor windows, they had no chance. Send for the glazers, new glass please.

He came flying down the track with a massive swipe and, err, a massive miss. Oops. Unlucky Tino. Stumped by Geraint Jones, the windows saved. I was in stitches, absolute stitches. I couldn't contain myself! It was one of the funniest moments of my cricket career. It still tickles me now.

The official record has it that I took 226 wickets as a Test match cricketer for England. Well, I think that's wrong. Surely sledging Tino out should be number 227? No offence, Gilo, but that one was mine!

But fair play to him – it wasn't all one-way traffic. I had another laugh after he was called up in 2012 to face England at Edgebaston, a couple of years after I retired. I just couldn't resist so I tweeted: 'The windows will be in danger when Tino's bowling!'

The windows were in danger that game – but only because he

creamed it everywhere! He smashed the England bowling to all parts: it was unbelievable. Bresnan, Swann, Finn – they all got hammered. But when he was on ninety five, he went for the windows again to make it 100. Oops.

But well done sir, that was incredible. Well done on your career, too. And well done for having me in stitches on a cricket field.

Just remember: mind the windows, Tino!

Freddie Flintoff
March 2015

CHAPTER ONE

THE PATH OF REJECTION

People love watching quick bowling. Are there ten guys in the history of the game who have bowled faster than me? No. Not many have. I've bowled balls of 98 mph. Who's quicker? Only Brett Lee, Shoaib Akhtar, Shaun Tait and Shane Bond in my era. Mitchell Johnson and I are the same speed. One ball I bowled for Yorkshire, live on Sky Sports, was 97 mph. It was an inswinging yorker to Neil Carter in a Twenty20 match against Warwickshire, around the wicket, and it ripped out his stumps.

I loved bowling quick – and I still do love it. It makes me feel free from everything. I'll be standing at the top of my mark. My mind will be blank, my blood's pumping and the adrenaline's going. The whole world is blocked out. I can intimidate a batsman, hurt a batsman, get them jumping around – and it makes the crowd happy.

I love hitting batsmen but I always check they are OK. I want to hit them in the head but I don't want to hurt them. Take an incident with the Zimbabwe batsman Hamilton Masakadza in 2013, for example.

I smashed him on the helmet and feared the worst. I was straight up the wicket to get to him first. I took his lid off and checked him over. Fortunately, all was OK.

Even still, my cricketing ability didn't please everyone. My father never showed an interest. To this day, he's never come to watch me play. I've played fifty seven times for the West Indies. He hasn't come to see one of them.

He knew I was playing on TV and he watched me on TV but he never came to the ground. Others had their dads in the crowd, whom they could look up to and wave to. They could speak to them when times were tough. But not me. Mine never even asked me to sort out a pass for him.

He's in prison now for dealing cocaine. He has struggled with cocaine, marijuana and heroin and has been a drug addict for over twenty six years. My dad has four sons, including me, but in my whole life I've only spent a week with him, once, when I was eleven. That was the first time I ever met him. We still talk – he's my dad and I love him but I haven't been to see him inside.

I did ask him once why it was like it was. I said, 'Dad, I played for the West Indies fifty-odd times. Why were you never there?' He said he was ashamed. Ashamed of what? He said he thought I was embarrassed by him. I wasn't. Not at all. He had problems – big problems – but my problem with him was that he never tried to kick the habit. I'll never judge my father but that got to me. He never even watched a school match, let alone a Test match.

It's sad but I tried never to let it affect what I did. I'd only try to let it inspire me; to fire me up. I had a strong family around me. I'd be at big games and I'd be able to see my mum or one of my aunts in the crowd.

My mum was one of five daughters. She brought me up on a maid's salary. She worked at a hospital, doing the laundry. I wasn't living in poverty but it's fair to say I grew up from humble beginnings. We weren't poor, that's for sure, but we didn't have a load of money to splash on cricket kit.

In fact, my first cricket shirt was a church shirt. And it was my dear grandmother – Marcia Best-Tait – who bought me my first pair of cricket spikes. Man, I loved them. I couldn't believe my luck when I got them. I wore them through the house every second I could, except it used to annoy the hell out of mum. The house we lived in had a wooden floor and I was putting holes in it every time I walked around. My mum used to yell at me, 'Please take them off!'

I used to wash them after every time I wore them. It was never a chore but even my mum used to get annoyed with me for that. She used to tell me it would make them weak so, eventually, I stopped. I didn't want to ruin my pride and joys. Most mums would be desperate for their son to be clean. Not mine.

So there was no Dad there but there was Mum. Other days I'd have my grandmother or my grandfather to support me, or my best friends. And there was one man who had been there and done it: my great Uncle Carlisle. Great Uncle Carlisle, my hero. He played eight Tests and twenty four one-day internationals for the West Indies. He hooked Ian Botham for six to get off the mark in international cricket from his third ball. He was my inspiration.

I must have been eight when my Uncle Carlisle was at his best. My teacher had the radio on and I heard he was whacking it around against England in a Test match. Wow. He was hooking the heck out of Devon Malcolm this time, who was bowling at the speed of sound. Devon is a national hero in England – and a good friend of mine. He's one of the quickest bowlers the country has ever produced. He took nine for fifty seven in an innings once against the South Africans, including the wickets of Gary Kirsten, Hansie Cronje and Kepler Wessels. It doesn't get much better than that.

But Uncle Carlisle was something special. He was hooking and taking him on, smashing it about. I just had to get there, so I did just that. I ran seven miles to the Kensington Oval stadium in Bridgetown, in my school clothes, and I had to persuade the security guard to let me in. 'It's my Uncle Carlisle batting,' I said. 'Please let me watch him.' And he did.

I didn't care how far it was. My uncle was the man of the moment. I got to the ground and the whole place was shaking. Then he did it. He hooked Devon Malcolm for four to bring up his century. Oh my God. Spectators invaded the field, lifted my uncle into the air and stuffed money in his pockets. At that point there, the seed was planted. I wanted people to chant my name. I wanted to carry this legacy on. I wanted to be a West Indian cricketer. I felt so proud that it was unbelievable. Devon went for 142 in 33 wicketless overs while Uncle Carlisle scored 164.

But I was always his nephew, or great nephew, as it was. Tino Best, Carlisle Best's great nephew. And, worse still, I was Carlisle Best's great nephew who wasn't good enough.

That had to change. I was sixteen when I signed up for the BDF Sports Programme in Barbados. It's for guys with sporting potential who also have an interest in joining the army. They take on young lads who are good at football, table tennis, boxing, athletics and cricket. It'd help me fulfil my dream to play for the West Indies, I thought. You're in there being prepared for war, working hard physically while also spending time on your specialist sport.

The army was an alternative career. I would have been a soldier. I would have done it and gone to fight for the British army. But opening the batting for the West Indies and following in the footsteps of Uncle Carlisle is what I really wanted to do. The army school was tough and was all about discipline. Yet on one day, as an eighteen-year-old, when I was to have my last chance to get into the Barbados Under-19 team, the rules of discipline cost me everything.

I had never played age-group cricket for Barbados because I was never good enough. I was among loads of hopefuls who turned up at the Weymouth Cricket Ground to partake in the trials for the Under-19s.

The ground was a big scenic stadium. On one side it had the transport board's bus terminal. One of the best education establishments – Harrison College – was on another side. A movie theatre – the Globe cinema – was there too and, in the distance, you could see the Queen Elizabeth Hospital. It was on the outskirts of the city but there was always a lot going on there. You'd get passers-by stopping and watching. People from work, doing day-to-day chores, would come over. A crowd always pulls a crowd. People were always having a peek in.

I spent the morning at the army camp and we all had to clean the facilities: the camp and the toilets. We'd all done our chores and the corporal was due to inspect at 3pm. It'd be simple enough: he'd check them over and we'd be off. Except I was wrong. One of the guys hadn't got his toilet clean enough. The corporal said he'd come back at 3.45pm.

The forty five minutes dragged but, eventually, I got out. I biked to the trials as quickly as possible. I was a man on a mission. The usual fifteen-minute journey took me eight minutes. I was a man possessed. I rushed to get changed and approached the coach to explain what had happened but he was having none of it. He was a real disciplinarian; real tough. He hated tardiness and I hadn't made a good impression. 'Leave,' he said. I protested. I told him I was part of the army programme and that I had to abide by their rules. But no – he told me to go.

It was painful. Agony. I'd worked so hard on my game to get this far and I couldn't accept it. I was a quick bowler who could make batsmen scared; a teenager feared by grown men. Then I started crying. I jumped on my bike to leave when Jason Haynes and Jason Parris arrived from school to have a practice. They were the big guns, the sure picks, the two opening bats. These boys were the top players.

Everyone in Barbados knew them. They asked me why I was crying. I told them but they didn't help much. 'Tough luck – such is life,' one said. I didn't like it. I told them I'd play for the West Indies before anyone on that field did.

I went home to my grandmother as down as I'd ever been. She told me, 'Tino, don't ever let anyone stop you. Don't let people control you. Go out there and fight.' My dad? He was nowhere.

Turned away before I'd even had a chance. Tino Best: Carlisle Best's great nephew; Carlisle Best's great nephew who didn't even turn up for a trial on time. The knockback hurt. All the hours of training and nothing to show for it.

Some months later, the South Africans came to tour the Caribbean. The tears had long dried but the memories were still raw. It was April 2001 and I had a chance, through the army programme, to have a bowl at them in the nets. Except this was South Africa playing against my West Indies: the team I was desperate to play for; the team my uncle worked so hard to play for. It would help me, I knew, but I didn't want to go. I'd sprinted seven miles as an eight-year-old to see my uncle score a Test century and I had left that day dreaming that one day the crowd would be chanting my name. I didn't want to help South Africa – the enemy – out.

But the BDF Sports Programme coach, Henderson Springer, convinced me I should go. He was a very tough man. His hallmark was hard work. His thing was that, if you work hard enough, you will always beat talented players. That's something he always strove for. So off I went, again to the Weymouth Cricket Ground, the place I'd been kicked out of a year earlier. There was no dirty toilet to stop me this time and, within minutes, I was in awe. Here were Boeta Dippenaar, Daryll Cullinan, Gary Kirsten and Herschelle Gibbs all warming up. These were superstars I'd only read about in magazines. Now I was about to bowl against them.

The South Africans were managed by an Indian chap at the time.

He brought us all in and asked, 'Who are the fast bowlers?' I said, 'Me,' and he laughed. The 5 foot 8 inches bloke could bowl fast? He wasn't humiliating me. It just wasn't normal. He was used to real, strapping giants.

I marked my run-up and took a deep breath. Gary Kirsten was facing: a legend with a game built up of pure grit, determination and immense concentration. He's a fine coach now; he was a fine player then. Kirsten played 101 Tests and finished with a batting average of over 45 and a top score of 275. Impressive. That's alongside 185 ODIs too.

I stood tall – well, as tall as I could. All 5 feet 8 inches of me was ready to prove a point. I took a deep breath and charged in. I bowled the ball as fast as I could, short and at his head. Then it happened. A huge clunk – it hit him flush on the helmet. The ball would have gone for six byes. He was stunned: 'Woah, who the fuck is this kid?' Kirsten was shocked. I'd made my impression.

I got back to my mark and bowled again, again and again, as fast as I could. I gave it everything. The batsmen were playing and missing. The other South Africa players were all watching. One of the coaches, Corrie van Zyl, had a baseball mitt. Except it didn't do him much good. I'd burst the netting of it with my pace.

After my spell, Cullinan called me over. Cullinan: 4,554 Test runs, a highest score of 275 not out with an average of 44. Like Kirsten, he was one of the best in the business.

'What's your name, young man?'

'Tino Best.'

'Are you any relation to Carlisle?'

'He's my uncle.'

'Oh, wow. How is Carlisle? You've got to send him my love and respect.'

This legend was actually talking to me? What the frig. Then it was Colin Croft's turn. He couldn't believe I was related to Carlisle.

'You're so quick but he was a batsman. How is this?' he said. This was Colin Croft speaking; a West Indies legend. He took 125 Test wickets and was a phenomenal bowler from wide of the crease. He was one of the four horsemen of the apocalypse. And at that moment, he was telling me I was the quickest bowler in the West Indies.

But Croft was upset. He couldn't believe I wasn't playing youth cricket for Barbados in the regional Under-19 tournament. He couldn't believe I couldn't make the army-programme team. I wasn't good enough for that, if I'm honest, because there were better guys, but he was shocked. Croft just couldn't believe I could bowl at 90 mph and I wasn't playing. 'Something's wrong with the structure,' he said. He thought I was a diamond in the rough. Coming from him, I was flattered.

The next day, I was back at Weymouth Cricket Ground. The army van, full of us hopefuls, pulled up at 7am. I was on a high. Hours before, I'd been praised by Colin Croft and Daryll Cullinan and it was about to get better. One of South Africa's leading bowlers, Makhaya Ntini, jumped on the bus and shouted, 'Where's Tito? Where's Tito? I want to see pace. Come on. Come on.' Word had already got around about what I could do.

I couldn't believe it. Here was one of the best pacemen in the world and he wanted to find me. I could sense a bit of jealousy from my friends. I mean, come on, Makhaya is calling my name. Well, kind of my name. I put up my hand and corrected him. 'Tino,' I said. 'It's Tino.' And with it, he welcomed me over.

We did two laps of the outfield and a few stretches when he was in my ear with advice. He wanted me to bowl quick; he was gassing me up to bowl fast. Allan Donald then came over. The man with 600 international wickets – a cricket great, not just a South African great. He was showing me how to hold the ball properly. What the frig. This is White Lightning. I was starstruck. I'd roughed up Gary

Kirsten and they wanted to see me bowl an old ball this time. They didn't want to get any of their batsmen injured.

I ran up and let the ball go quicker, quicker and quicker again. I was living a dream and Makhaya was impressed. He invited me to chill out at the pool in the hotel with them after. He told me not to give up. He said, 'You're quicker than me. You're going to make it.' Graham Ford agreed. He told me I was the quickest he'd seen in the Caribbean. He said he would like to get me to Natal, where he coached, as I'd be a real handful on the South African pitches. I was a kid, he had a series to win and concentrate on, but he wanted to know me. He showed an interest in a boy not good enough for the Barbados Under-19 team, or the army-programme team.

A few days later, Ford went on my uncle's radio show: *The Best and Mason Show*. It was hosted by my Uncle Carlisle and a chap called Andrew Mason. On the show, Uncle Carlisle asked Ford if he'd seen any good young players while he'd been over here. His reply? Me. 'Your nephew, Carlisle. He is super talented.' He asked if I'd been making runs and Ford said, 'No, he's not a batsman. He's a bowler.'

Uncle Carlisle couldn't believe it. We hadn't caught up since I'd joined the army programme, such was the nature of the environment we were in. Real communication with family and friends was minimal. Before, I had been a batting all-rounder who bowled a bit of medium pace but the programme was a tough one. We were lifting weights, doing sprints, working hard every day. It made me. I went from being a medium-pacer to a young man with a weapon. Graham Ford continued, 'Carlisle, he's got a real gift. The cricket board in Barbados must take a look.'

In the end, I got to play a part in the Test series. I worked pushing the sightscreen back and forwards in Barbados. South Africa went on to win the series 2–1. I must have knocked Kirsten's confidence because he never hit top form and ended up averaging twenty five.

Cullinan, meanwhile, averaged fifty one. Makhaya took seven wickets in four Tests and it was in Barbados that we said our goodbyes. He called me over for a pic and it's one I still treasure now. After that, we exchanged letters. He kept encouraging me.

With Ntini's kind words in my ear, I played in a Pro-Am event – the Fred Ramsey tournament – a few months later. Teams come over to Barbados for a round-robin festival. I was playing for the Keith Medlycott XI and there were some English players over with us: Ed Giddins and Gavin Hamilton. Giddins played four Tests for England, while Hamilton played thirty eight ODIs. I did OK and seemed to impress them. They couldn't believe how quick I was. They told me I had talent and that I could make it.

Word soon started to get around even more. They'd bigged me up – Graham Ford had in the national media and the South African team were full of praise too. So the Barbados Cricket Association gave me another chance. I was twenty when I was called in for another trial match. Where? Weymouth Cricket Ground, of course. The place I'd impressed the South Africans so much – and the place I'd been refused a trial because of a dirty bog.

There were thirty guys there, all trying to get in the Barbados squad. I couldn't sleep the night before. My palms were sweaty. I knew this was massive. Fidel Edwards and myself were both there, opening the bowling, trying to make the grade in the biggest game of our lives. Batting were Sherwin Campbell and Dale Richards. Both were considered class acts.

I steamed in again, just like I'd done to Gary Kirsten and just like I'd done to Daryll Cullinan. But it all went wrong. I got smoked. I bowled too full, then too short, but what could I expect? I'd never had specialist coaching. I didn't know how to bowl an outswinger. I had no control and was just express: a Ferrari without a steering wheel.

The selector was Calvin Hope. He told me that I had talent and that I had pace but that I just needed to get some coaching. 'We're going to cut you but don't give up hope,' he said. I was down but not defeated. There were net sessions in the week to go to and I'd make sure I wasn't going to go away. I wanted to show how keen I was.

Off I went to the nets that Wednesday. I bowled Sherwin Campbell, the best batsman there. I hit him on the shoulder then knocked his stump out the ground. Sean Armstrong, who went on to play first-class cricket for Barbados, was batting too. I did the same to him. They came over and asked, 'Why didn't you bowl like this in the trial game?' Nerves – it had all been down to nerves.

Sherwin was the captain of the Barbados team and he wanted to give me a chance. There was another trial game later that week, where the squad went down to fifteen from twenty two. He told me to bring my boots and whites. 'Someone always breaks down in critical matches,' he said. I was having none of it. I didn't want to go. I was embarrassed. Why would I want to? I wasn't good enough.

Any time off needed to be granted by Sergeant Dave Sobers, the man in charge of our army programme. I went back to camp the next morning at 7am to explain the situation but there was never going to be too much of an issue. Sarge was a good man. He told me to believe in my ability and go but on one condition. If I didn't play, I was to go back to camp straight away. No problem, Sarge.

The venue: the Weymouth Cricket Ground. Where else? I watched the first session, then the second. It was tea-time and I was beginning to accept that my chance was over. I'd be back to the grind; back cleaning the toilets. A career in the army beckoned. Not that it was the end of the world. I wanted to be a cricketer, yes, but the army wasn't all bad. I'd be a soldier and live in the UK, or be a pastor. My grandmother had always been very religious and I'd grown up around the church.

But then, in those seconds before tea, I got my own gift from God. Ian Bradshaw was charging in when he felt his hamstring go. He was a good bowler, was Ian. He went on to play sixty two ODIs for the West Indies and five Tests but it wasn't his day here. Off he came at tea-time and that's when Sherwin came over.

'Did you bring your boots like I told you to?'

'No,' I replied.

Sherwin got angry.

'Did you not hear what I said? I told you to bring them.'

'I haven't.'

I was embarrassed. I didn't want to be the guy who was so desperate for a game that he'd brought his stuff. After an agitated Sherwin got angrier, I put my hands up and admitted that I had actually brought my boots, so off he went to one of the selectors. The man was Clinton St Hill, who I knew from Pickwick Cricket Club. He used to play in his day and said I was good to go on. 'He's just going to bowl crap and get smoked,' he thought. 'Of course he can go out there to make up the numbers.'

God had given me a chance but I needed another favour. I stretched at the top of my mark, focused on the job, then I began to pray: 'God, I don't ask you for much. Just can you help me once in my life? Just calm me; give me the energy of calmness. Let me show people what I can do. That's all I'm begging you for.'

And I bowled and bowled and bowled, from the first over after tea until just before the end of play. I was a fit boy – I could get seventeen on the bleep test – and I bowled at the speed of sound. Jeez, I must have been close to 100 mph. I got through fourteen overs in a row – that kind of spell is unheard of nowadays – and I took three wickets. Everyone had come out to watch me.

At the end of play, off I walked, to applause from West Indies wicket-keeper batsman Courtney Browne, and Sherwin Campbell. Sherwin came up to me and said he'd never seen anything like it and that I had earned the chance to play for Barbados. On that Thursday morning, no one had known me – on Thursday night, everyone did.

I came off and said I was ready to bowl again. That's when they called me Animal. The nickname still stands now.

I called Sergeant Dave Sobers to tell him I'd be playing the rest of the game. Man, I was proud. He was a top man. He wished me good luck and told me I didn't have to report to camp. The next morning, I opened the newspaper at breakfast. There was an article written with Gavin Hamilton and Ed Giddins that a local journalist, Barry Wilkinson, had done at the Pro-Am tournament. They were raving about me. I turned two more pages and there I was again in another article, this time on my performance at the trial game. I was bowling at the speed of sound, it said. Woah.

I ended up with four wickets that game, which would prove to be one of the most important of my life. I still had to find out if I'd made the final fifteen so, a few days later, I was back on my bike to ride down to the Kensington Oval to hear my fate. As I approached, out came Barry from the press room to congratulate me. I'd made the squad. My heart was pumping from the adrenaline I felt: was this a dream? I got back on my bike and headed straight to my grandmother's in Richmond Gap.

Her house was an oldish one. It had one or two leaks but it wasn't the worst. The toilet was out in the backyard and you had to put a towel or a rag over your head whenever you needed to go, to keep you dry. She had three bedrooms – one of which I stayed in – and she raised chickens and ducks in the garden. Looking after them was one of my Saturday chores. She was out the front when I got there and I just ran to her to squeeze her. She started crying. Never give up, she had told me. I hadn't. Here was her reward.

I told my aunt, my grandfather, my mum. My mum's house was across the road and I used to live between hers and my grandmother's. They were all made up. I told my Uncle Carlisle – I couldn't wait to let him know. His advice was different. 'This is the start of a new road for you,' he said. 'Now you've got to maintain this, get into the final

XI.' He was really laying down the nitty gritty. He'd been to the top and he knew what I had to do.

I couldn't wait for the 7.30pm news and, as expected, I was across the TV channels. Everyone knew the name. Tino Best: Carlisle Best's great nephew who was now good enough for Barbados.

My dad? He was probably in prison. But everyone now knew me. Tino, Makhaya, not Tito.

CHAPTER TWO

SEX, DRUGS AND FATHERHOOD

I have four loves in my life: my mum, my son Tamani, my daughter Thalia... and Melissa.

Melissa was my everything. I met her walking home from the Samuel Jackman Prescod Polytechnic institute in Bridgetown when I was fifteen. I was there wanting to learn another trade, learning about cars. It was a secondary interest – cricket was always my main one. On one quiet walk home, this young girl turned my world upside down.

I was window shopping, as teenagers do, when I saw Melissa and a group of four friends hanging around the shops. Man, I couldn't believe my eyes. Melissa was the prettiest girl I'd ever seen. I'd fallen in love. I just had to go over to speak to her – so I did. I was never shy on a cricket field and I was never shy off it.

One of her friends said how cute I was but I just wanted Melissa. She was just the prettiest girl I could imagine. Our eyes locked together and we were totally in awe of each other. She must have admired my handsome looks and I admired her gorgeous face. I introduced myself and we swapped numbers.

For two or three hours each evening we would talk on the home phone. My mum used to get annoyed that she could never use it but I didn't care. I had, in that single moment, fallen head over heels in love. If ever there was love at first sight, this was it.

She was in the upper-sixth at school at the time and I courted her; took her out for dates and eventually made her my girlfriend. From the moment we started going out we had big dreams together.

On 15 November 2000, one of those dreams became a reality. I was nineteen when we had our beautiful baby boy Tamani. It was one of the happiest days of my life. I was outside the hall at the hospital waiting for news of his birth. My grandmother came out and told me, 'You have a boy.' Wow. I would have loved a daughter the same way but I always wanted a son as my first born – and I'd got one. As soon as Melissa cradled him in her arms, you could see he was the whole of me. He was the spitting image – except better looking! Life couldn't have been better.

I was young but having Tamani was so right for both of us. He calmed me and he made me more responsible. He gave me drive and he made me more focused on what I wanted to achieve. In fact, he is one of the main factors behind me making it as an international cricketer and, more importantly, making it in life. I wanted to break into the Barbados team to earn money to put a roof over his head. I wanted to be the one he could always come to with his problems. As his dad, I may have had dreams to turn into a superstar cricketer but I wanted him to know I'd always be there for him. I hadn't had that father in my life but Tamani sure would in his.

I thought Tamani, Melissa and I would spend the rest of our lives together. Melissa and I had a family and a beautiful relationship. Everything was rosy. It was, anyway, until I messed it all up. I will put my hands up now and admit I was the problem. Not her, me. We'd had so many dreams and I ruined them. We were going to get a house together, move in together and live together forever but it never happened.

I'm not proud of it at all but I cheated. I cheated, for a bet, to show off to my new Barbados team-mates. That moment of stupidity cost me the love of my life. It still haunts me now.

I'd just broken into the Barbados squad in January 2002 and I would have done anything to impress my team-mates. I wanted to show I could bowl express pace, I wanted to knock stumps out the ground and I wanted to smack the ball out the park. The Barbados team was full of big stars. I was a young kid eager to please.

And, as men do, we talked about girls. There was a stunning girl who was quite well-known – let's call her Becky, although that's not her real name – who worked in the media. After one practice session in Bridgetown, all the boys were talking about her. Courtney Browne, Ryan Hinds and Floyd Reifer were three big players at the time and they were all marvelling over how hot she was.

It was then that the challenge came down. Courtney turned to me and said, 'Tino, I bet you can't pull that chick.' I hadn't played a game for Barbados but I wanted to be one of the boys. Me, being my cocky little self, wanted to prove them wrong. 'I can pull her easy. I can get that anytime,' I said. And there it was.

I had a beautiful baby boy and I had a girl who was my everything but here I was, going home to write a handwritten love letter to a girl I'd never met. I sprayed some of my Hugo Boss aftershave on the paper, folded it in half and put it in a smart envelope. The next day, journalist Barry Wilkinson came down to interview me before our next game. I gave him the letter and told Barry to give it to Becky. 'Cool, bro,' he said. An hour later, Becky was calling me.

The bet wasn't even for any prize or anything like that. I just wanted to prove that I could do it. I answered her call and we hung out. We saw each other more and more, started having sex and I didn't tell the guys anything. Fame and popularity had gone to my head. I was in with a beautiful media personality, who was even more popular than me.

But soon it all came crashing down. The tabloids had got hold of it and we were in the gossip column of the national newspapers. I'd been caught. One of the waiters or waitresses had ratted me out to the paper and I was crapping myself.

Melissa confronted me. The paper hadn't named me but she just knew. She was angry and she had every right to be. She asked if I'd been seeing Becky and I never, ever lie to Melissa. I put my hands up and admitted I'd done it for a bet. It was guys playing around, I said. She asked if I'd slept with her and I apologised. She knew.

She cried her eyes out. She was so disappointed. Tamani was so young and I'd risked everything we had. She told me that cricket had gone to my head and blanked me after that. And you know what? She was right. Becoming famous had happened too early. The Caribbean islands have a real laid-back culture and I suddenly had girls starting to chase me. I don't think I'm a bad-looking guy and the girls were after me because they wanted to date a guy who was popular. I did get drawn into that.

I'd cheated on my girlfriend. I was having sex behind her back and I'd left her heartbroken. She told me she couldn't even watch the news without seeing Becky's face. I apologised. I was so, so sorry. I wished it'd never happened but it had.

My mum was disappointed, to say the least. My whole family were. I'd cheated on the mother of my son. I'd won the bet with the guys but I'd given up the love of my life. When I saw the guys the next day, they gave me a big ovation. 'Animal, you are the man. You are the man, Tino,' they said. But they didn't know what was going on in my personal life. They didn't know about Melissa. Then, when they did, they told me she'd get over it; that she'd take me back when I started getting wickets, or when I got a call-up for the West Indies. They were wrong – we never reconciled.

I respected her decision to cut me off and I will always have love for her. It hurt me but there was nothing I could do. I have a huge amount of respect for Melissa now but she's moved on. She still speaks to me and she's never, ever stopped me from seeing my son. There was just no sex and no loving in that way again. Her family are hugely respectful and still call me to see if I'm OK. They are fantastic, loving and welcoming. I love them to this day.

Tamani knew we weren't together but he knew we both always loved him. I guess that's the only thing I can learn from the situation. I'd never want my wonderful son Tamani to get himself into the situation that I did. Only now, reading this, will he know why we broke up.

I ended it with Becky after that. It was never going to work. She was physically attractive and, at a different time, it would have been great – but it was just not right. She didn't know I was still supposed to be with the mother of my son, for a start. It just wouldn't have had a future.

To be honest, after that, I was a pure playboy. I was a man whore. Not that I'm proud because it means the woman I love doesn't want me anymore. The West Indian boys, in general, are more promiscuous and laid back and I always used to enjoy myself on tours. That's not to say I don't want to get married, because I do. It won't be for a few years though. Until then, the women will have to wait!

The West Indian culture is a relaxed one, in that we'll never be told to marry into this race or to that person. All my family say is that I must respect women. I should have respected Melissa more and I still miss her now. But she's had another baby boy now and is with her new partner – and I have to move on too.

Together we have Tamani and he's an incredible young lad. He's fifteen now, very responsible, very passionate and, yes, he plays cricket too. His full name is Tamani Tino Best. Tumani, in

Africa, means 'warrior'. I liked the name but swapped the U for an A because I felt it looked better. Hopefully, it still means the same thing!

My Tamani is a warrior, so it's appropriate. I wanted Tino in his name as I want him to be a champion. I love my name – Tino la Bertram Best. It's the one thing my father gave me that I'm grateful for. I love him for that. Bertram means 'great'. So it's like Tino, the greatest, Best.

Melissa lived with her mum and I lived with my family growing up, so Tamani was between houses. Tamani and I have always been very close but, like all fathers and sons, we've had arguments. There's one I really remember and not because it was bad but because my boy made me proud.

We had a petty disagreement and he went at me, saying, 'Dad, I don't need your help to do anything.' I was taken aback. He told me he was going to make it on his own; that he was going to be a fighter. I want to hear him say that. I want my son to fight – and he does. I'll help him through his life and he knows that but he has an inner steel that I'm so proud of.

Unlike me, Tamani's a batsman. He's a classy left-hander who opens or bats three. However, when he failed to make the Barbados Under-15 team, he called me crying. I told him straight away to keep working hard and to battle. He went away and in the next two innings scored forty five not out and forty nine. I was so, so proud. He wiped his eyes and went and scored some runs. It doesn't get better than that. I was never going to be given handouts from my Uncle Carlisle and I don't want to give them to my son either. He tells me he wants to be better than me. It's a great goal for him but I've told him, 'You can be but, if you want to be better than me, you must work harder than me.'

I love going to watch him play cricket. I've been there whenever I can to see him. Sometimes, with me being his dad, he has to cop a bit of stick. He went out against a school in Trinidad and they said they'd bowl bouncers at him. 'Your dad used to hurt people. We're going to too,' they told him. But Tamani has a lot of character. He told them they must have never seen his Uncle Carlisle play because he was going to hook and pull them like he did. Tamani has watched YouTube videos of Uncle Carlisle and he knows all about his great innings through the years. What a thing to say.

He's not shy of a word, Tamani. And if dads are the ones who are supposed to embarrass their sons, no one told him.

The Zimbabweans came over to the Caribbean in 2013 for a three-match ODI series. We dominated them, with Dwayne Bravo in exceptional form, averaging 172 across his 3 innings and ending up the leading wicket-taker with 10. I only took three wickets but didn't go for many. Tamani came to watch one of the matches. He was there at the Kensington Oval, sitting in the Greenidge and Haynes Stand with his school mates. I was so proud that he could see me playing for the West Indies. He'd been to games when he was much younger but wouldn't have really known what was going on.

The spinner Shane Shillingford was bowling and he duped the batsman to get them to send a catch up in the air. Now this was an absolute dolly. It was the easiest catch ever in an international game; one of those you could take with your eyes shut. Except I got underneath it and dropped it. It was so easy. Everyone was stunned. What the hell was going on? No one could believe I'd dropped the ball. The crowd were rocking and then, suddenly, it was stunned silence. Except from Tamani.

He stands up and yells out, 'Dad, dad, dad!' What was he going to say? Some consoling words? No chance. 'You've just dropped an absolute dolly,' he shouts. It was the funniest thing I've ever seen. The whole West Indies team dropped down laughing. Oh my God, there's my son slagging me off! It was absolute vintage. Darren Sammy was in hysterics and Chris Gayle was holding his belly, laughing his head off.

'Bobski, your son has just dissed you!' they joked. Bobski was another of my nicknames that my old team-mate Rashidi Boucher gave me, after my love of Bobby Digital from the Wu-Tang Clan, and the name just stuck. The lads found Tamani hilarious and I told him I'd give him some lashings when we got home. All in good spirits, of course. Just to see him in the crowd that day felt so amazing. He will always have seen his dad play for the West Indies, dropping easy catches…

Tamani is a talented cricketer and I hope he follows in my path to play for his country. He's had his knockbacks but I've had them too. It's how you bounce back that makes you into the man you want to be. He's ambidextrous, which always helps, so he can use his left and right to the same level. His off-spin with his right looks a bit suspect – a little bit of a throw – but his left-arm pace is decent, although I think he'll be a batsman. His ambidextrous talents come from my dad but they must have missed me.

OK, Dad couldn't have done much about that but there were plenty of things he could have. He was a real disappointment for me: doing drugs, ending up in prison and never being there for me. He was addicted to crack cocaine for thirty years. I love him but he never took the fight. He never battled against it. He just gave up.

Throughout my childhood, I didn't really have an idea who he was. I hardly saw him. He cheated on my mum and she kept me away from him. My mum Yvette was a real tough cookie and she totally protected me from all the crap. As a kid, my grandmother Marcia played the mother role. She was incredible in the way she looked after me and brought me up. She was the mother and my mum was like the father.

With my mum having four sisters, it was good having all these women around me to help. They were all so supportive and I have an amazing relationship with them all to this day. If I had any questions about finances, they'd be there. If I've got girl problems, they're there.

Even when I grew up and started to earn a decent wage playing cricket, my mum would always give me advice. People said I should build a house for my grandmother and mother after breaking into the West Indies team but, in truth, those people didn't know who I was or what my family wanted. I built a wonderful home in Christ Church – four bedrooms, a swimming pool, a really smart place – and I invited my mum to come to live with me. But she had no interest in that whatsoever. She wanted to stay in the house she'd lived in since 1994. She wanted to live in the house she'd brought her kids up in. I ended up paying towards her apartment there instead.

She told me to just concentrate on playing my cricket. She kept me grounded; told me to make my money and build a house afterwards. 'You could break your hand, get injured and lose your career at any time,' she said. The house could wait. I took her advice, built a house when I was twenty six and now I have no mortgage. My mum always knew best.

My grandmother raised her five daughters and she was phenomenal. Her children are too. They're beautiful, articulate, strong women. She did a great job with them. My dad had three other sons: Shawn and Bertram, who are both older than me, and Jamone, who's younger. I met Shawn and Bertram for the first time when I was eleven and my dad's troubles affected them far more than me.

Two years ago Bertram told me a story that will always stick with me. He lived a stone's throw away from his primary school but used to sit out on the wall as a kid when he was done. The teacher once said to him, 'Bertram, why aren't you going home?' His reasoning still makes me emotional now. He saw all the other kids being picked up by their dads and just wanted to be like them. He wanted people to think his daddy would pick him up but dad never came. Bertram's a big man with a young son now and it still affects him to this day.

The emotional strain on Bertram and Shawn was massive and when Bertram told me this, I realised how lucky I was and how much of a good job my grandmother, mother and aunts had done. I got away lucky. I always had food, clean clothes and a roof over my head. My auntie Margaret hasn't any children and I was her first nephew. She used to take me all over the country, and then there were my other aunts: Delores would take me to fayres, Olivia had a salon that I used to hang out in and I used to love play-fighting with Ancilla. She was the youngest and always used to snitch on me if I'd been naughty at church! She got me on the front page of the *Nation* newspaper once as a cute kid holding some fruit. They only picked me because I was so photogenic!

All four aunts had different characteristics that helped me become the person I am. These women kept me strong and resilient. They kept my head up when times were tough. They made me strong and they taught me the ethics of life. What they drove into me was simple: respect. When I walked the streets, I'd make sure I was polite to everyone. They told me to keep my clothes clean and my mouth out of the gutter.

And I had a cricketing idol who was also my great uncle, Carlisle. He was my grandmother Marcia's brother and was almost like a father for me too. Growing up, he was always taking me to Empire Cricket Club to spend time with his team. He put the cricket bug into me.

I knew my dad was on drugs and I suppose, if I was of weaker mind, I could have followed. Not that that was ever, ever going to happen. My mum and grandmother raised me to be tough and peer pressure was never going to sway me. People I knew were smoking marijuana but these guys weren't my friends. That's what was great for me: I used to hang around with the right guys. I was too into cricket and knew that drugs would never help me with what I wanted to achieve. I was Tino Best: the boy who wanted to play for the West Indies. Drugs would kill that dream. I had three main cricket friends: Ryan Paul, Ryan Haynes and Fernando Paul.

They were top schoolboys; well-educated lads. We all stayed on the right path.

I want my dad to act as an inspiration to my son. Tamani knows his grandfather's in prison. I want him to use it as a reason to make sure he strives for excellence at every opportunity he can. I've said to him, 'This is not what you want to be.' Not because I don't love my father, because I do, but because he's where he is today. It could have been brilliant if he was around but he wasn't and I've just dealt with it.

My brothers have given up with him now. He just mugs them off and they've written him off but I haven't had the emotional agony that they went through, so I'll continue to try to help him out as much as I can. The problem is that, if I give him money, he just buys drugs. If I give him clothes, he sells them for drugs. If I give him a bike, he'll sell it for drugs. I can't give up on him and I'll keep fighting. It pisses me off when he sells things I've given him but you can't choose your family.

At times, people in society have looked down on me and laughed at me because my father's a drug addict but it's not my fault I'm his son. You can pick your friends but you're born into your family. People would say that I thought I was someone but that I was nobody because my dad was a druggie. But they're wrong. I am somebody because God gave me talent and grace. The taunts used to bother me but I'd just call mum or my grandmother up and they'd big me up and I'd soon forget it. Now I just ignore it.

People in cricket have made jibes about my father too. A couple of years ago I was playing a game against the police team. One of the players taunted me about my dad being on drugs and in prison. He picked the wrong man. He made me angry so I bowled a bouncer and fractured his hand. I won't say his name but, when he reads this, he'll know who I'm talking about. His hand was in a cast for a few weeks after that.

On my mum's side of the family, I have two half-sisters: Toni and Tanisha. There were so many strong women around me from when I was born – and in 2012 another came into my life.

After Becky, I dated some high-profile girls but never settled down. I started becoming Tino Best: a household name that played cricket for the West Indies. Girls would come up to me and people would scrutinise and dig up the past. Life became harder but in 2010 I grew close to a nice girl in Guyana called Shonette. I'd known her for years. She was beautiful, of Amerindian descent, with lovely eyes. I was immediately taken aback when I saw her. To be honest, it felt like meeting Melissa all over again.

We dated, she came to Barbados and we enjoyed a decent relationship. In 2011, she fell pregnant and, on 14 July 2012, we had a beautiful daughter, Thalia Gomes. She's a little handful, who loves her mum, dad and her big brother Tamani. Unfortunately, the distance meant it was never going to work with myself and Shonette. But God gave us a wonderful daughter and I'm blessed for that.

CHAPTER THREE

TALKING THE TALK

Sledging is an art – and I love it. Cricket is about fine margins and, if you can get under a batsman's skin, boost yourself and get an advantage through your mouth, so be it. It's all part of the game.

I've been sledging – and getting sledged – since I was ten years old. It all started when I played tape-ball cricket at the St Leonard's Boys School, a mile and a half away from my house. It was a huge tradition in Barbados. We'd get a tennis ball and put white electrical tape on it to make it an extra ounce and a half heavier. It'd skid off the concrete pitches we played on so fast. It felt like it was going a million miles per hour.

A whole group of us would play every Sunday inside the schoolyard from 10.45am until 4.30pm. It was a concrete yard, there was no grass pitch and you'd bat once. There would be twenty-odd fielders around you: five slips, two gullies, fielders everywhere. It was packed as everyone wanted to bat. The ball was firm and, if it hit you, it stung but we'd wear no pads. No helmet either, of course. Just a box to protect your nuts.

There was one guy by the name of Glenroy Corbin. I'll tell you now, he used to bowl a tape-ball quicker than Shoaib Akhtar bowled a hard ball. Man, it was fast. He used to say he'd hurt me if I didn't stay in line. If I backed away, he used to pepper me. He was a good man, always helping with technique and advice, but it'd be tough cricket. At that time, I used to bowl medium pace. From the age of six to eighteen I wanted to be like Gordon Greenidge, Desmond Haynes and my Uncle Carlisle. I wanted to bat for the West Indies like them and hook the fast bowling for six.

I was ten or eleven when I played against these lads twice my age but they didn't care. They used to give me stick for being Carlisle's nephew. 'Let's see if you are a good hooker like Carlisle,' they would say. There was one time I scored sixty not out as a twelve-year-old for my school, Garrison School, in an Under-15s match against Harrison College. I came to the tape-ball game bursting with confidence. My uncle came and collected me that Sunday morning and asked how many I had made. I couldn't wait to tell him.

I went in to bat against a guy called Sylvester. He was from one of the villages nearby. Man, he could bowl a tape-ball real quick. He let go of the first one so fast and the ball hit me in my jaw. Ouch. I started to cry but they didn't care. The fielders were on me, telling Sylvester to hit me under the ribs and give it to me. They could see the tears but it didn't matter to them.

My uncle was playing first-class cricket at the time but he would be playing in this match too. He was at first slip, telling me to watch the ball. 'Lil' man,' he said, 'keep your eye on it. Don't turn away.' I was trying but, when your eyes are full of water, it's not easy. I was always confident as a kid: it's what my grandmother told me to be. I was feisty too, probably because my father's absence had some kind of effect. Uncle Carlisle knew what I was like. He always used to tell me my mouth would get me into trouble and to expect some serious bouncers.

I didn't stop. Of course I didn't: I wanted to battle. I faced eight more balls before the next guy knocked me over. I walked back to cover to field, crying. No one cared. I was annoyed, too. You'd only get one chance to bat – unless you bought someone's hand for ten dollars – so that was that for the day. Three hours for a blow in the face, all in front of my hero; my idol uncle.

Although it wasn't all bad. I got to watch my Uncle Carlisle bat after me. It was 1993 – three years after he scored 164 against England – and, of course, he was still a top player. There were fielders everywhere but he didn't worry about them. He batted for forty minutes. With the twenty-odd fielders having a go, attacking all the bowling is completely unheard of. They bowled loads of short balls but Uncle Carlisle just loved hooking. So do all of us West Indians – we love it short and quick. He smashed them, just like he did to Devon Malcolm when he made his Test match ton.

He always commentated on his own innings too. It was incredible. When I was younger, I didn't really pay much attention to it and only when I got older did I understand what it meant. Playing a Test match, commentating on his shots, brilliant! I remember thinking, 'Oh my God, my uncle is so cool'. He used to count every run as well. He's an accountant – an economist – so he's very good with numbers.

One time, when he was playing for his club team, the Empire Cricket Club, he had an argument with the scorer. Mr Dean was his name. He used to do a great job but he upset my uncle. He came off one Saturday and Mr Dean said he was 101 not out but my uncle was adamant he was on 105 not out; that he'd missed a boundary. He said, 'Mr Dean, you can't trick an economist; you can't steal runs from me.' It was all done in good spirits, in a jovial way, and the next day Mr Dean apologised to my uncle. He'd gone home and worked out his mistake. He hadn't put down a four.

Uncle Carlisle drove me back home after that tape-ball game. He told me I had to watch the ball longer. If I didn't, I'd get hit and, if I got hit, he said, the other players would laugh at me. He was very hard on me as a youngster but he was toughening me up. He told me, 'Tino, you want to be a great cricketer, but great cricketers don't cry.'

It was tough and I sat there, silent, agreeing with him. He was right and all I wanted to do was get his respect. That was my greatest motivation. He was always on at me. Even when I got into the West Indies team and, in 2012, scored ninety five against England batting at eleven, he rang me to cuss me. He was fuming that I'd thrown it away and got out. If only Mr Dean was scoring, he might have missed four or five runs!

Sledging was part of growing up but I'd never be personal. I'd tell a batsman they couldn't bat. I'd tell a player they couldn't hit a cover drive off the next ball, or hit the spinner over deep midwicket. They'd say the same to me too. Sometimes they'd say they'd give me ten dollars if I hit the next ball for four – and I would. It was great fun. You'd get money for playing well off the dads who were watching the tape-ball game. It was awesome.

I sledged when I batted as well. 'If you were any slower, you'd be late for your own funeral,' was a good one. I'd try and wind the bowlers up as a kid so they'd bowl short. That's what I wanted, then I'd rock back and hook like my Uncle Carlisle. I was always strong on the hook and pull.

I used to be sledged on the pitch and teased off it. The dynamics changed when I went into the army sports programme at sixteen. I couldn't get into the top six as a batsman, as they were all better players than me. I was laughed at. 'The best thing about you, Tino, is that you're not even the best cricketer in your family,' they said. It angered me, made me curse and I wanted to fight them. I had a short fuse but I put that down to my dad never being there. I always had to defend myself. Of course, I didn't fight – it would have put me in military jail for the night – but I wanted to.

I took that negative energy and tried to channel it into something positive. I had to train harder, so I began lifting weights and working for longer in the gym. If I couldn't hurt them by fighting, I'd hurt them in the nets. I'd bowl short balls and make them fear me. I was eighteen when I started to bowl real quick and I got these boys jumping around. At twenty one, I'd broken into the Barbados team but, for the first season, I never sledged. I was finding my feet.

I started to give it some in the second year. I'd walk past batsmen and say, 'I'm going to break your rib, mate.' I'd tell them, 'I'm going to cut you,' and stuff, just to get under their skin. Batsmen used to complain to the umpire and say I was threatening them. Not that I minded too much. I was just a young quick with no care in the world.

That Barbados team had the likes of Sulieman Benn, Courtney Browne and Floyd Reifer. These three were serious players. They all played for the West Indies – in Tests and ODIs – plus they had hundreds of first-class games between them. They used to chip away in the slips, saying stuff like 'Come on, Animal, I need some fries and ribs.' They were talking about the batsman's ribs, of course. This was normal. Barbados loved their quick bowlers.

There was a time when Michael Clarke told Jimmy Anderson he'd get 'a fucking broken arm' in the Ashes, which got picked up on the stump microphone. So what? If I was batting, I wouldn't have minded one bit. Just make sure that, when you're bowling, you hand it back out to them. You have to be tough to play Test cricket.

I was selected to play my first Test against the Aussies in 2003, long before Clarke became captain. I found out I was playing in the morning and I rang Brett Lee's room to tell him, 'Binga, I'm starting today!' I loved the man. I first saw him back in 2001 on TV and I was taken aback with how much of an athlete he was. The way he ran in, the whole body mechanics he has, it's amazing. He's one of my favourite cricketers. Once, we sat in Trinidad for an hour and just chatted about fast bowling. He's a rockstar. He congratulated me and said see you later.

When I was batting, I hit a shot over his head. He was up in my face, telling me he'd break my fucking ribs. I loved it. I remember thinking, 'Yes, this is awesome!' As a bowler, you have a cricket ball, the batsman has a bat. It's part of the game. If I bowl you a bouncer, hit it – hit it for six, or for four – or defend yourself. You've got a bat, use it. At the end of the game, we sat down and he gave me advice on life as a quickie. No hard feelings, just a huge desire to win.

And yes, there have been a few occasions where it's all got a bit out of hand. I was playing in the Caribbean Premier League in 2013 for the St Lucia Zouks. It's one of the biggest Twenty20 tournaments on the planet. A load of the big names were there. We played Shoaib Malik's team – the Barbados Tridents – and I got him out twice. Shoaib grew up playing tape-ball cricket, like me. He's a Pakistani who has a decent record in international cricket. He's played thirty five Tests but found more success in ODI cricket, playing well over two hundred games with a batting average in the mid-thirties.

The next year, one of the guys I knew told me their game plan was to give it to me; not to let me bully them. If I talked, they were to give it back. So it was me against Malik again. He hit me for two fours and went at me. 'Come on,' he shouted. 'Bring it on. Go for me.' He basically said he wasn't afraid.

I went back to my mark. I'm pumped and he's pumped. The next ball he shuffled across his stumps and I bowled him – and I let rip. I clenched my fists and said, 'Go inside, you cunt.' Now I know around the world it's used differently but cunt is a normal word in Barbados. We'd use it regularly. Malik flipped. He turned and snapped at me, 'Don't call me a cunt.' He was raging. I could see it in his eyes. I told him he's in Barbados and to get out of my face and that's when he put his arm on me. It wasn't aggressive, he didn't push me, he just touched me.

We both got fined for the face-off, which was fair enough. I mean, I don't think anyone should lose money but that's how it is. If anything, it should have only been him fined, as he was the one who made physical contact. After that, it all kicked off again. His missus got involved, saying he should have lashed me. She tweeted that night,

'Racial abusing on a cricket field?disgusting.i knw @realshoaibmalik didn't hit him but how I wish he would hav! #tinobest #idiot'

What the frig? Was this real? This is cricket. What happens on the field stays on the field. She said I said something racial. No way did I. His wife plays tennis professionally, apparently. Sania Mirza is her name. I'm told she's a good doubles player but I only know a few players: Serena and Venus, Maria Sharapova as well. I was going to say, 'Do you actually play?' but I thought I'd leave it out. What was it to do with her anyway? Her husband hit me for two fours, after all. I decided to leave it and not get involved in a public slanging match.

What really annoyed me was her claim that it was racial. No way was it racial. A cunt is a cunt. At the end of the game I shook his hand. They won and I thought that was that. Clearly it wasn't. I've played him once since that game in St Lucia. I got two or three wickets but I didn't get him out.

I don't mind Shoaib Malik. His record speaks for itself. He's a decent T20 cricketer. Decent but not one of my favourites. I don't have any problems with him. I just think his wife trying to get involved was not on. He's a decent player of medium pace or swing but I think he has a pea heart when it comes to quick bowling. He doesn't get in line much. Then again, when it comes to 95 mph bowling, there's not going to be many people who fancy it.

That night it kicked off again. We went back to the Hilton hotel and I encountered Kieron Pollard. He was the Tridents captain, who has made a big impact in the West Indies. He's six foot, six inches tall;

I'm five-foot, eight. We were just about to get in an elevator when he came up and poked me in the face. He may have been a foot taller than me but I wasn't having it. By physically touching me, he got my back up. He said I thought I was a tough guy. I didn't reply – then I lost it. I retaliated. I punched him on the shoulder and he kicked me back on the leg – and we had to be parted. Lucky it wasn't at the army camp – I'd have been put in prison!

I'm not bitter now. There are no hard feelings. I was just really disappointed that Polly did that, as he has a very high IQ. He's a good person and I've got a lot of respect for Polly but I think that, because of his size, he thinks he can bully people. He tries to intimidate people who are smaller than him. You have to stand up to someone like that. That's what my grandmother always told me. 'Always respect people,' she said, 'and, if people disrespect you, keep out their way.'

He didn't get to land a proper one on me because Darren Sammy held him back and Liam Sebastien held me. We've shaken hands since and that was that. People like to gas that it was a big altercation – it wasn't. We got parted. I don't regret it, although I do think it's a reason why I didn't get a contract in the Caribbean Premier League (CPL) in 2015. He's a big player in that tournament and I think that incident ruined my reputation a little bit.

The army programme always taught us to defend ourselves and to never back down, so I didn't. God is good and God knows I didn't do anything wrong. My family weren't interested either. It was something and nothing.

Kieron Pollard, as a cricketer, is a good ball hitter. He's a Twenty20 player. I think he's a swashbuckling batsman who can bash Twenty20 bowling but I don't think he's got a particularly great technique. If T20 didn't exist, we'd never hear about him. It'll be hard for him to play Test cricket as the two formats are just so different. Test cricket really puts you under the microscope. You could bowl short at him, then back of a length and then bowl a fuller one and he will nick off. I'm an OK bowler but, when James Anderson, Mitchell Starc or Brett Lee charge in, you can't survive without a good technique.

Physical contact is wrong but I think sledging is great for the game. It's entertainment. It's what makes cricket so exciting to watch. I'd say stuff to a batsman but it'd never be personal. I'd draw the line at that. I'd swear, yes – 'He's the worst fucking batsman I've seen in years,' or, 'I shouldn't be bowling at you. You should be making ketchup!' – but never personal, just cricket.

I remember sledging Graham Thorpe at Sabina Park in my second Test match. I didn't get any wickets in the first and it was twelve months until the second, so I couldn't wait for it. I was bowling heat: 92, 93 maybe 94 mph. Sabina Park was rocking. It was jam-packed; sold out to capacity. Of course it was – the English were in town. I'd already hit Marcus Trescothick and Mark Butcher in the head when the room attendant came into our dressing room and told us the English were shocked by me. They couldn't believe how quick I was bowling, he said. All I could think of was to gas it up even more and give it all I had.

Even Graham Thorpe was backing away. Graham Thorpe: 100 Tests for England, 6,744 runs, a best of 200 not out at an average of 45. I gave it to him and he replied, 'Oh, Besty, I've faced all the greats, loads of better bowlers than you. You're nobody.' I wasn't happy. I told him I'd hit him in the head and put some sense into him. So I went round the wicket and steamed in, bounced him and he hooked. He got a top edge that flew to fine leg and Adam Sanford was there to catch him.

GP Thorpe. ct Sanford b Best. 19.

My first Test wicket. I'd got under the great man's skin. Everyone was chanting, 'Tino, Tino, Tino.' The whole place was just one whirlwind of energy. I've never felt anything like that before in my life. When I got him out, I couldn't stand. I fell straight to the ground because my knees just went weak. Here was little Tino, from Richmond Gap, who used to tend to his grandmother's chickens, getting a Test match wicket in Jamaica. I felt like Muhammad Ali.

There are a few other incidents I will always remember. We went and toured Australia in 2002 when Glenn McGrath let rip at Ramnaresh Sarwan. Now, I like Sars. He's very tough and I found the way he left international cricket very hard. He's a fantastic human being and a fantastic cricketer but McGrath went at him. He asked how Brian Lara's private parts tasted. After a while Sars got tired of it and told Glenn he should ask his wife. Glenn just flipped and lost it. He was absolutely spewing.

I don't think what Sarwan did, in that moment then, was wrong. It wasn't nice that Glenn's wife was ill and it was incredibly sad when cancer eventually took her in 2008. I don't know if he knew that back then but you can't be personal like Glenn was. If you get personal, be prepared to take it back personally. If he'd told Sarwan he couldn't bat, or was going to nick him off, then fair enough. If Sarwan told him he was the worst bowler he'd faced, again – fair enough. It's when it gets personal that it's all wrong.

I used to like a run-in with the Aussies. In 2005, I was twelfth man for the last Test of the series in Adelaide. Fidel Edwards got Justin Langer out for ninety nine. Brilliant. I remember I was bringing the drinks on and I couldn't help myself. As I passed Langer, I shouted, 'Yesssss!' He stopped as he was walking off and was furious. You have to pass their dressing room on the way back and he was waiting for me. He asked me what I'd said and I told him. Again, he wasn't happy. 'You're a prick, mate. You're a prick,' he said. He said he'd complain to our coach Bennett King about me.

Bennett was an Aussie himself. He worked in a very Australian way and he didn't do me much good as a coach. So, if Langer was going to snitch on me for that, I wasn't too bothered. I laughed and said, 'Do you think Bennett is going to give me a lashing? Come on, man.' Then it all died down and after the game we had a Foster's together. He's a top man, Justin. A great batsman too. It was said in the heat of battle.

But there are a few cricketers you just don't start with. Kumar Sangakkara is one. Just never say anything to him or he will bat like a man possessed. Tillakaratne Dilshan you can sledge a bit and get under his skin, Mahela Jayawardene too, but not Sangakarra. Adam Gilchrist is the same. Leave Gilly and don't say anything to Rahul Dravid either, as he's a god.

Brian Lara is another you leave alone – not that I knew it when I was younger. I bowled two short balls at him in a first-class game and went down and told him, 'I'm going to pin you up, mate.' Courtney Browne came over and told me to stop the chat, as he doesn't even want to bat. Sometimes Brian was like that. He was very relaxed and quiet and, if you gave him some, he'd focus more.

The next ball Brian played a square cut that went off his bat like a bullet. The next was a big extra cover drive. Two balls, two fours. In the next over, thank God, Corey Collymore nicked him off. It could have been a long day otherwise. In the second innings, I got him out, nicked behind and said nothing but slid on my stomach. It was the craziest celebration and I never sledged Brian Lara again.

And then there's Kevin Pietersen. Now, I've never been intimidated running in against a batsman but with KP it was different. He was crazy. I've never bowled at someone that big and with that presence. I'd always want to give him a single and bowl at the other guy. That's very unlike me. He's the most intimidating player I've played against in my whole career. Ian Bell would be scampering for his life when I played him but KP was just a giant.

Another English batsman, Nasser Hussain: I used to love bowling at. I loved sledging him too – and I could because I knocked him over so much! In 2004 I bowled him a few times. I wasn't afraid of Marcus Trescothick or Michael Vaughan either. I used to get under Trescothick's skin but KP, in the one Test I was up against him, was different.

It's funny how people round the world have different personalities. The easiest to wind up are the Indians. They're very sensitive, especially away from India. At home, where the pitches are flat, you just don't say much to them. But, if we are in the Caribbean, or in a different tournament elsewhere, you can get under their skin easily. One or two of them have a go. You can give Virat Kohli talk and you know he's going to go back at you. Rohit Sharma is the same. They're so confident and don't respect many bowlers. The others are a little weaker.

It can get pretty serious with us. In the Caribbean we take it to breaking point. If you're not strong, you won't succeed. On many occasions, guys say they'll bite a batsman's hand. By that they mean 'take his girlfriend'. When a batsman is seeing an ex-girlfriend of a player, they know about it and will be given hell. They'll be saying 'another man's garbage is the next man's treasure' and all that. Guys were furious but I didn't get involved in that. I'd tell them I'd break their heart or their ribs but really I was so quick that I didn't need to intimidate. Not personally anyway.

Sometimes sledging can be funny too. There was one moment when we were playing the Windward Islands and their number three was facing me and kept playing and missing. He was horrific. Sherwin Campbell piped up from second slip, 'Hey, mate, I see better bats in a cave.' Everyone dropped down laughing. I was running in as quick as I could, the serious fast bowler, and even I found it funny. The batsman must have done too.

All the chat got to me at times – more on Freddie Flintoff and his 'mind the windows' jibe later. It was a way of putting me off but I loved it. All the guys playing international cricket are super talented. It's the mental capacity that makes or breaks you.

CHAPTER FOUR

RECRUITING

I'm a broken boy, bawling my eyes out. The tears won't stop. Tears of pain, tears of agony, tears of heartache flooding down my face.

Five weeks into the eight-week recruiting stage for the BDF Sports Programme it's all got too much. It's the pathway to sporting success or a career in the army. You have to be recommended for the chance to get in and only the most talented are wanted. Except that we're away from family, we're away from friends and I'm a sixteen-year-old boy who's, by far, the youngest in the group. Get me home. Get the baby home. Sat in front of me is Corporal Knight: a real military man; an imposing figure. I cry, cry and cry – then begin to pour my heart out.

I was homesick. I missed mum, my mates, the home comforts: I missed everything. I had just sat and watched the cricketers play because I couldn't make the team. I wasn't good enough. This was it – the end. I'd joined the BDF Sports Programme to work hard, become a man and play cricket for the West Indies. It was never going to happen.

Corporal Knight begins to talk. Suddenly, he calms me. I'm the youngest recruit ever, he says, and I'm on the brink of something so special. Making it through the recruiting stage and on to the BDF Sports Programme is where I want to be. He knows I'm broken so he delivers the words that pull me together.

'Do you know how proud your mother Yvette will be when she sits down at the pass-out parade?' he says. 'How proud will she be to be the mother of the youngest-ever recruit? Three more weeks Tino. It's just three more weeks.'

Even at sixteen, I knew what I wanted. It was either a career as a professional cricketer or a career in the military. Be a warrior on the cricket field or a soldier on the frontline. While there, we'd be educated well, which was nice, but I was a sportsman-in-waiting. When I first met Commander David Dowridge in December 1997, at the funeral of my friend Aaron Barker's grandmother, I didn't need much convincing to join.

I'd gone to support my good friend Aaron, who was in the BDF Sports Programme himself. He was three years older and played table tennis and cricket there. They were two of the five sports where talent was identified: football, athletics and boxing were the others. Aaron was a decent cricketer: an off-spinner with a beautiful action and a good lower-order batsman. He was a bright boy too, well into his academics, who attended Harrison College.

Aaron had already explained the recruiting process so, when Commander Dowridge told me about the programme, I already knew what I was letting myself in for. Even so, hearing Dowridge tell me I had the potential to play for the West Indies, after watching me play for the Garrison School and my club Pickwick, put a spring in my step – even if I was at a funeral. It's always nice to hear that someone has watched you in person. I may have been the young school kid but the old wise-head Dowridge had done his homework.

You had to be seventeen and five months to join the Sports

Programme. I was a full year younger, meaning they had to ask permission from my mum for me to join early. Of course, she said yes. This was an opportunity for me to focus and follow my dream. Her little lad was on his way.

The interview stage was a pretty easy one: Did I really want to do it? You bet I did. I wanted it more than anything. Then it was medicals – pull-ups, push-ups, strength tests – to determine if I was fit and strong enough. I passed, obviously. My fitness has never let me down.

If the first day at a new school is hard, the first day at the BDF Sports Programme is brutal. I – and twenty nine others – arrived at St Ann's Fort, one of the main bases, looking the part. I had a full head of hair and I was wearing a long-sleeved shirt and tie, long trousers and my beautiful black shoes – nice and sharp. Dress to impress is what my Auntie Margaret used to say. She was a needle worker who made all my clothes as a youngster. I didn't wear Armani, Dolce & Gabbana or brands like that as a kid. I was all about wearing the clothes made by my auntie and trying to make them look a million dollars.

Everything around me was pristine. The sidewalks were white, the lawns well cut, the trees well-watered. We lined up and, one by one, were given our military numbers, so I barely had time to marvel at them. 'Recruit Best,' Corporal Fleming pointed at me. '9822114.' 98... 22... 11... 4. Round and round in my head it went. 98... 22... 11... 4. I was joining the military. This was happening. Woah. I was standing in a military base, bristling with excitement because I'd never been in one, and I had an actual military number – 98... 22... 11... 4. Round and round it went.

But soon the eagerness, the enthusiasm and my hair were gone. All the boys had been sent to the barbers to get skinheads and my little pretty-boy afro was off. If I thought that was bad, worse was to come. With us all still wearing our smart shoes, nice shirts and fresh trousers, the Corporals started to make us run. Are these people insane? Why are they making us do this? Then out came the fire hose. They soaked us and made us keep going.

Three hours passed and we were still running. What the frig? Run, push-ups, sit-ups, then another run: all in our best clothes. I couldn't believe how they were treating us. I wanted to go home. This was inhumane. I want to play elaborate drives, slog sweeps and hook and pull the quick bowlers. But at the same time, I was sixteen and carefree, running on adrenaline, loving the challenge, hating the pain.

At lunch I looked at the other twenty nine. I looked into their eyes; I looked at their body language. 'He wants to drop out,' I thought. 'And she does. And that other one to my right, he's going to drop out too.' As that food came out, never has lamb stew, mashed potato and vegetables tasted so nice. Then the cake and the ice cream too. Oh my God, that food was so good.

But deep down, I knew this: we were on a military base and the hard work had just begun. We had barely taken our last bite when the sergeants got us out for more torture. This time it was relentless sit-ups on full stomachs. Guys were vomiting, girls were vomiting. I couldn't believe what I was seeing. I couldn't believe recruiting was this serious. In front of my eyes, people were in pieces. This was the army.

That day was the start of the toughest eight weeks of my life. After a trip to the military store to be given our camouflage uniform, we were given a lesson in how to make our beds. Even that was hard graft. The corner of the bed had to be at a 45° angle to the sheets. You made the bed military style. It was strange but I loved it. I knew I had two long months of this and I couldn't go home. I could make one phone call a week. The toughest of challenges but brimming with excitement, this was it.

Day one was hard, day two was harder. Before we'd even had a chance to settle into a good sleep in our bunk beds, the lights were on. It was a Sunday: the day to chill and relax. No chance. The Corporals had come in at 4.30am to wake us. Corporal Fleming was in charge of my section, Section One. 'Everyone get the fuck up,' he was shouting. 'Morning to you too, Corporal,' I thought. 'We're going on a run,' he continued. A run? Who were these people? Were they crazy?

So at four thirty in the morning we were running through the villages. Five miles out, five miles back. It was the craziest thing I'd ever experienced. Then it was time to wash, have breakfast and change into our military uniforms. They had to be pristine. The boots had to be shined. If they weren't, you'd be punished. If anyone had any stubble on their chin, that was it: a hundred straight push-ups.

And, like all soldiers do, we had to drill. The corporals beasted us as we marched: left, right, left, right, left, right, HALT. And again. Left, right, left, right, left, right, HALT. From 8am until noon it was relentless. Two water breaks were a chance to rest our tired ankles and feet. Every march had to be perfect. 'What the hell is going on?" I thought. 'What the hell is this recruiting stuff?' I barely had time to think before we started again, like a bowling run-up, perfectly timed: left, right, left, right, left, right, HALT.

Sometimes my halt wasn't good – and boy, was I told. Corporal Fleming was soon in my face, yelling, intimidating. 'You, babyface, your name is Bamm-Bamm.' I asked why. 'Bamm-Bamm is the baby in *The Flintstones*. Do you understand what I'm telling you?' I had no choice but to understand. If I didn't, he'd give me push-ups until my arms collapsed. With another brutal bark, Corporal Fleming was back into me, demanding my military number: 9822114, Best, T. He was satisfied, just. 'I've got my eyes on you boy. You're lucky,' he snapped. I'm shitting myself. Welcome to the Programme.

Over the days that followed, our routine was the same: running in the morning, breakfast, then four hours of drilling. In the afternoons we had to go and do an etiquette class taken by Major Reece. He was a real tough-looking dude. He used to tell us we could never be a pro athlete if we couldn't use a knife and fork properly. How would we eat at a state gala if we couldn't eat right? I learned lessons from him that stayed with me a lifetime: which piece of cutlery to use and when, which one was the sherry glass, the wine glass, the champagne glass, the water glass. From table manners to knowing the ranks of the military officers, knowing who to salute and who not to salute, military law: he made sure we knew what we were doing.

But even Major Reece's know-how couldn't save me from a few bashings. If you do something stupid in camp, you're going to be punished – and I was no stranger to getting my knuckles rapped.

Every day we had to make sure our military greens were in top-notch condition. They had to be washed, well-pressed and starched sharply. The starch stiffens the fabric after ironing and is used to make the clothes look more professional. Cleanliness was a must in the camp. We used to have locker inspections, toilet inspections, bed inspections – you name it, they inspected it. Everything about recruiting was the need to be clean all the time. And, if we weren't, we'd be punished.

One day, I fell foul of the rules. Corporal Fleming came in and looked through my locker, as he always did. He didn't like what he saw. One of my shirts had a mark on it from where I'd forgotten to wash it. He tore into me, saying, 'Recruit Best, you've got a nasty shirt in your locker. I'm going to bash you, boy.' With the rain pouring, Corporal Fleming sent me outside carrying a bunk bed on the top of my head. He made me spin like a helicopter, while holding the bunk bed in the air for an hour and shouting, 'Ninety eight... twenty two... eleven... four. I am recruit Best, T. I am a dirty recruit.' The whole camp was watching me. Military officers walked past with a smile on their face. Then, when I looked over, they'd tear into me and ask what I was looking at.

Everyone had their fair share of being bashed. There was a really good athlete there. But she was rude one day and paid the price. The corporals made her wet the entire barrack square with a shoe polish tin. The square was massive and there she was, wetting it bit by bit. From midday to midnight she was there, doing the most pointless of tasks.

Another time, they made one of the cricket guys sweep the entire square with a toothbrush. There was a reason for their harshness. The corporals used to want to break you, then mould you into what they wanted you to be. They used to defeat you with the simplest of things. They were preparing us guys for war. You can't have a soldier on the frontline missing home, weak in body and weak in mind. I was being taught confidence; the need to believe in myself, and that mindset is still embedded in me now. I worked hard then, before I was anything. Without that, I'd be nothing.

As if we needed proof that this was true military life, we had to look no further than our time in the bush. We lived there for three days and three nights, hiking, sleeping in tents and living off biscuits and cheese. We had to dig trenches to the sides of our tents so that, when the rain fell, it wouldn't flood them, and we learned the art of map reading. I saw some centipedes in the woods that were the size of snakes. Man, it was crazy.

One night during those tough weeks of recruiting, I woke up at one in the morning, in bits. The physical pain and mental strain had become too much. My grandmother always told me God would help me through the toughest of times, so I decided to pray. The barrack room had a balcony and I made my way out there to look up to the stars. 'I just want to get through this, God,' I said. 'Just help me get through this.' It was all I could do. I needed his intervention.

Each of the three sections of our barracks had corporals: Fleming, Knight and Pearce. Fleming and Pearce were real tough, no-nonsense men but Knight was cooler and I used to like him a lot more than the other two. He had a real personal side to him.

For all Fleming's hard-nose regime, he did help me learn some life lessons. He got us to play this game where we were all lined up in a row, numbered one to thirty. Fleming would say something to the first man in the line, who'd pass it on to the next one and so on until it got to the end. Fleming said stuff like, 'There's a farmer who has six cats and five dogs.' But by the time it got to number thirty, it would have changed to something bizarre. The farmer would be called Benjamin and have a castle, and there'd be no mention of his cats or dogs. Fleming preached not to worry about hearsay; to make sure you get the truth yourself and don't listen to rumours. So, as a sixteen-year-old kid, I knew never to take notice of any doubters. It's a lesson that still stays with me now and one that all came down to my upbringing in the military.

Beyond the runs, the pain, the early mornings and the agony of camp, us thirty recruits bonded real close as a group. The guys I were sure would drop out stayed and we got real tight. Not one of them left. We used to sit down and talk to each other about what we wanted to achieve. We were all brought together by the need to go places. None of us wanted to be remembered as someone who did nothing.

My greatest memories from those days are of sitting in the barracks square with my good friends Rondell 'Crashy' Pollard, Ricky Barns and all the other recruits. We'd talk about our goals. We'd go round and spell them out, one by one. Some wanted to be the best footballers who played in the Premier League, others wanted to fight in the army – and then there was me. When the chance to speak came round, I'd tell them, 'My name is Tino la Bertram Best. My father named me la Bertram because he wanted me to be the greatest – but he's barely in my life. I've been brought up by my mum, aunts and grandmother and my biggest inspiration is my uncle, who played cricket for the West Indies. I've joined the BDF Sports Programme to play first-class cricket. Then I WILL play for the West Indies.'

The others would poke fun at me. They used to laugh that I couldn't make the BDF cricket team. The girls would say I was too good looking to be a cricketer and that I should be a model instead. I loved them all deep down and I think everyone loved me. They appreciated that I was an honest, straightforward kid with goals to go big.

Even with the support of the others, the eight weeks were real tough. When it got hard on a ten-mile run, these fellow recruits were the ones who inspired me home. Close bonds were formed and it made it so much harder to witness their suffering the more I knew them. I saw Stephen Howell, another man made of steel, cry so hard because he missed home. Richard Morgan, a fellow recruit, fainted because he was being bashed too hard. They made him do 500 burpees, which are basically squat-thrusts and then a jump, and it all got too much. These boys were hard as nails but even they struggled.

Despite the physical torture, cricket-wise I was benefitting. I became fitter and stronger as time progressed – even if it wasn't enough. I was on the bench for the cricket team all through recruiting because I wasn't good enough. I used to go to the coach after games, tell him I trained the hardest and ask why I couldn't make it into the team. The reply was simple: keep grinding. So I did. Deep down, I knew I wasn't worth a place in the team.

For those few months I was the water boy. I was not even seventeen, with my baby face, and I guess I had so much to learn. But I always strove for so much and I wanted to be a soldier going into the heat of battle on the field – not just off it. I would do the chores, mix Gatorade for the other bowlers and pay my dues. Away from the cricket field I lifted weights for hours. As a result, I began hitting the ball further. I was a batsman who bowled off-break, or medium pace, remember. Bowling wasn't my forte but, when I did chuck a few down, they were coming out faster and faster. This military thing was making me strong; a real man. I was bowling a hard, quick ball and something serious was happening. I was in the process of becoming a 90 mph bowler.

If I hadn't gone through that recruiting, I would never have played for the West Indies. I doubt I'd even have played for Barbados. I put all my success down to that. God put me in a position to test me. If I'd have rebelled against it, I would have failed, but I didn't. God opened up my talent and that's where it happened for me. I would go from an eager boy to a strong man.

I still see some of the guys from the programme now. Most of these have made the transition to the army to become soldiers and fight. We still have a close bond and, no doubt, always will. One of the guys, Corey Clarke, has gone on eight tours to Afghanistan with the British army. He's seen things that I daren't even imagine. I met up with Corey a few years ago and he told me he was so proud of me and what I'd achieved. He wanted to know what I'd been doing but I hated the fact he was asking these questions. Why should he? He was the real hero. I told him to forget me because he could Google it. I wanted to hear about him: his life in the military and what he'd done. I'm a soldier of cricket. Corey is a soldier of war. He's saved lives, that man. I have so much respect for him.

In the end, the early mornings, sleepless nights and hard graft was all worth it. Corporal Knight promised the pass-out parade would be brilliant and he was right. All our family and friends were there and I was brimming with pride. We marched together – left, right, left, right, left, right, HALT... And again: left, right, left, right, left, right, HALT. The guys and girls who had become my close friends were all around me: united as one.

We marched and turned to face our loved ones together. When I looked, there was Tilia: my stunningly gorgeous good friend who had come to support me. And then I locked eyes on Mum, with the biggest grin on her face. There it was, there and then. My mum's pride etched all over. With no dad, I guess I had it tough but imagine what it was like for her as a single parent bringing me up. She always wanted me to do something positive; to be a positive force, unlike my dad. She'd just watched her first-born son pass-out through the army. I'd made her proud. I'd gone from Recruit Best to Pioneer Best.

During those two months the seed of determination was planted. I sit around now and look back, remember the tough times and how it was all worth it. Would modern players be able to get through it? I don't know. Freddie Flintoff and Darren Sammy would. They're real tough cookies. But would everyone? I doubt it.

The only other cricketer to have made it out of the scheme with success is Miguel Cummins, a quick bowler for Barbados who played an ODI against Ireland in 2014. As good as it was, my rise to fame annoyed some and I began to get frustrated with life in the BDF.

When I made the West Indies team, some of the guys around the place used to get jealous. They'd speak to me differently, start picking on me and digging away: little things, like trying to tell me my shoes weren't clean and things like that. It used to get to me. I think they would open the papers, see me and want me to be all high and mighty so they could have it out with me. I'm sure it was all down to jealousy.

Even as an international cricketer, I still used to play cricket for the BDF side at the weekends. I had my West Indies gear and some just didn't like seeing it. One of the cricketers hit my West Indies helmet in with my bat. It was pure jealousy. Another time my bat was taken to bang in a locker in the barracks. The only people there were cricketers and I knew it was one of them. It couldn't have been anyone else.

I had it out with the group and told them that whoever had damaged my gear didn't respect people – then I flipped. I smashed the barrack-room phone into a million pieces. It was the only way people could communicate with family and friends. If they were to disrespect me, I'd hit back at them. As plans go, it wasn't my greatest.

My godmother, Ometa Lopez, was on me straight away, pointing out that it was government property and that I was destined for trouble. She was right. When I got back to camp, the military police were waiting for me: 'Mr Best, you're coming with us. You've damaged government property.'

They told me I would be going to court. Tino Best, superstar of one Test match at the time, could now be ending up in jail. The police sergeant was a good one: Sergeant Rowe. He talked sense and knew that people had been getting under my skin. 'You need to be smart and walk away,' he said. If only it was that easy.

I was frustrated and angry. I got to court on the Monday morning and the major presiding over the case started to lecture me. Us two had a history and never really saw eye to eye. She told me I had no right to smash a government phone just because I played for the West Indies but it wasn't like that. I felt that what I had worked hard for was being disrespected and I told her I'd smash ten more phones if the same thing happened again. Not my wisest words.

My courtroom sledging didn't go down well. She told me my arrogance had annoyed her and she confined me to two weeks in the barracks. I could play cricket and train but I wasn't to go home. Imagine that elsewhere. Can you imagine someone telling Alastair Cook that he couldn't leave somewhere? Or Mitchell Johnson that he was not to go home? Whether on the cricket field or in a courtroom, I'm never shy of a word or two. My decision to ask why the rest of the cricket team hadn't received the same punishment wasn't my best one either. Shut your mouth or it'll be a month, she said. I bit my tongue.

I felt the people in charge at the BDF Sports Programme wanted to humiliate me. I was told to sweep the road outside the military camp for my punishment. Yes, outside, not even within the confines. Normal people in their cars would drive past and toot their horn and shout stuff like, 'Tino Best, get back in the West Indies team.

Stop sweeping the road!' They asked me what I'd done to get this punishment but I would just smile. Inside I was seething.

I had put the BDF Sports Programme on the map but I felt disrespected. Rules are rules but I felt this was a harsh penalty, especially when the guy who damaged my stuff got off scot-free. No one ever owned up to doing it but I know who it was. If you're reading this, I know who you are.

In August 2003 there was more trouble. One of the corporals told me to go and clean the toilets and that really got to me. I'd been there over five years. I'm not trying to be a big-time Charlie but this was a rookie's job – and the corporal knew it. I spent hours, days, weeks even, cleaning and mopping in my early days there and I felt I was above it. I objected and the corporal hit the roof. He said I thought I was God's gift to cricket and that I'd never make it back in the West Indies team. Fortunately, he was wrong.

I couldn't hold my anger in and my response to tell him he'd never achieve anything didn't go down well. I got a week's confinement for that. It was around that time that I called Commander Dowridge to explain everything. I was honest with him and he was honest with me. He felt I was outgrowing the Sports Programme and becoming too big for it. 'You've excelled so much and you've put us on the map. Now it's time to go,' he said. So, after five and a half years, I was off.

Only the back end of my time there was sour and I'll always have to deal with that disappointment. I'm sure I was the same then as I was at the start but some people just didn't like it. I was an international cricketer, earning nice pay cheques and I had the money to get good things. My clothes may have changed, there were more interviews in the papers and on TV but I was still Tino Best. Recruit Best turned Pioneer Best: 98... 22... 11... 4.

CHAPTER FIVE

LIFE IN THE FAST LANE

Fast bowling is like a superpower. It gives you a feeling like no other. The adrenaline pumping, the ball in your hand, the mind totally blank: fast bowling is a drug. It can put you on a high, it can have you on a low, it can hurt people. And it's addictive.

It's dangerous – and that's why I love it. I like hitting people. I love the sound of the leather ball smashing the helmet and hearing that clunk. I'll never tire of hearing that noise: the massive thump. If you hit one batsman, you don't just rough up him, you rough up the whole team. It sends a psychological message to the rest of them that this guy is bowling fast and that's what you have to do.

I've put countless guys in hospital. One, in Bermuda, was left with twenty four stitches. Did I feel bad? No – because he was good. I've broken about five hands, five forearms and broken a few toes with crunching yorkers. I've broken some ribs too. In December 2015, at the age of thirty four, I hit the Windward Islands opener Miles Bascombe in the head and he had to have fifteen stitches to sew his ear back together. Fast bowling is a weapon.

It's a nice feeling seeing that physio come running out. That's the game; that's how it is. That's what bowling is all about: intimidation. I'll hit someone and the boys will tell me, 'And again, and again.' It'd be the same if one of us was hit. If I hit someone, the next ball is never, ever going to be pitched up. If I've hit you once, I'm going to try and hit you there again.

I was playing a first-class game in St Lucia in 2004 against the Windward Islands. I steamed in, as I do, to bowl to Craig Emmanuel and hit him so hard in the ribs that the ball just stopped dead and dropped on the pitch. I'd broken five of his ribs with the same ball. A year later, in 2005, we were playing a List A game against Guyana in Barbados. Derwin Christian was batting. He's a wicket-keeper batsman who played a couple of Twenty20 internationals for the West Indies. I ran in, bowled a bouncer and broke his collarbone. The ball didn't stop that time. It flew off for four, taking just the one bounce before it went over the boundary.

It's a batsman's game now. The bowlers need every bit of help they can get but, at the end of the day, I'm a human being. I'm a cricketer, yes, with the desire and passion to win every time I take to the field. But I'm a human who never wants to do any long-standing damage. If I hit someone, I'll go and check up on them and see if they're OK. It's the first thing I want to do. I like to bowl fast and I like to intimidate but cricket is just a game.

We were all reminded of that at the Sydney Cricket Ground in November 2014. Phil Hughes was batting for South Australia in a Sheffield Shield game against New South Wales. Now Phil was a young player with huge potential. He'd already played twenty six Tests and twenty five ODIs for Australia and had the world at his feet. He was so, so talented. When Michael Clarke said he'd play a hundred Tests for Australia, I think he was right.

Phil was sixty three not out when he went to pull a bouncer and got hit on the back of the neck. Sadly, two days later, on 27 November, he died. The incident was an absolute tragedy. Rest in peace, Phil, and condolences to your family and friends. You were doing something you loved doing – and something you were very good at.

But we all must remember that this was an absolute freak incident. Cricket has been played for God knows how many years and no one had died. It wasn't the pace of the ball that killed him either. Phil was actually through his shot early because the ball wasn't that fast. It just hit him in the wrong place and it cost him his life. It saddened me so much but I wasn't shaken up, as such. Put it this way: it wouldn't stop me from bowling a bouncer, that's for sure. I wouldn't want to bowl a bouncer and kill someone but there can be no blame on the bowler that day.

I've hit Brendan Nash before, who played twenty Tests for the West Indies and faced some of the fastest bowlers in the world, and left him in hospital. I hit Jim Troughton too, who used to play one-day cricket for England, and left him with a nasty gash. Batsmen get hit but never, ever to the extent that they die. It was a massive freak accident.

As a cricketer, you either have the natural ingredients to bowl pace or you don't. It's not something you can just coach. The make-up of a fast bowler is a unique one. It's not all about height to generate bounce, like some people believe. I'm 5 foot, 8 inches tall, remember, and that hasn't stopped me bowling 98 mph.

So what goes into a fast bowler? Well, here's what I think are the key qualities.

A fast bowler's body is similar to that of the best sprinters. Both are born with fast-twitch muscle fibres that optimise their explosive performance. There are those athletes who can run marathons and they are brilliant beasts. They have the best endurance but they won't have a chance of beating Usain Bolt in a sprint – and that's all down to the fast-twitch fibres.

Desire is huge too. Every cricketer – batsman, bowler, wicket-keeper – must have desire. If you don't have desire, you won't accomplish anything. It's the same in any workplace. There are those who have the desire to go to the top, and those who don't and they fall by the wayside.

The next essential feature is technique. You have to make sure that your head is dead still at the release point and the leg must be braced so you can bowl over it. The body goes through the mill and that's why I had to work so hard in the gym. For me, the strength-and-conditioning guy is the most important part of a cricket team. The best bowlers have to be kept in the best physical shape. It's about combining ab work, clean and jerk lifts, dead lifts and sprints to activate those fast-twitch fibres. At the BDF Sports Programme I wasn't the most talented cricketer so I knew I had to work hard in the gym to give myself any chance.

If you've got a good strength and conditioning regime, fast-twitch muscle fibres, guts, desire and a real heart, you give yourself a chance. You've got to be prepared to have sleepless nights because your legs are hurting, your back is sore and your body is in bits. It's not just the batsmen that feel the pain of fast bowling.

When I started to whizz it down, I was told I would be the next Malcolm Marshall. Everyone wanted to be him as a kid. So did I but I modelled myself on all the greats. Wayne Daniel was the quickest West Indian I'd ever seen bowl and I couldn't believe how fast he was. Wayne was a great bowler and a great person.

Technique-wise, I also turned to baseball for help to see how they did it. I watched guys like CC Sabathia, who played for the New York Yankees, and Randy Johnson, who played for the Seattle Mariners and Arizona Diamondbacks. Their throwing accuracy and power amazed me. Cricket can learn a lot from baseball players. I wanted to know how they trained, studied their technique and made sure I was doing the same strength and conditioning work as them.

As for cricket, there were two other guys who inspired me to bowl fast: Brett Lee and Shoaib Akthar. Wow. I watched them as a kid and they just bowled so, so quick. It made me want to be just like them. Everything about them astounded me. The excitement in their faces, the way the keeper would have to jump high to take balls: it was something else.

Shoaib was one of the stars of the World Cup in England in 1999. He was man-of-the-match against New Zealand in the semi-final and ended up taking sixteen wickets in the tournament. I watched him, astounded. Batsmen just couldn't touch him, he was that quick. You can probably understand why it meant so much to me when I met him in 2005.

By the time I introduced myself to Shoaib, I'd been playing Test cricket. He knew who I was. 'Tino, let me see you bowl fast,' he used to say. You see, fast bowling is like a brotherhood, which is so welcoming. If you can bowl at 90 mph, you're in a small band of people in the world. We look out for each other. Fast bowlers have the same unique characteristics. We know what it's like to experience the pains, the struggles and the pressure we put on our bodies. I think that's why we are always so close.

At first, I didn't even know I could bowl quick. It was only when I got through a spell at the Central Cricket Club in St Thomas – in the middle of Barbados – that I realised it could be an option. I'd got into the BDF Sports Programme and Henderson Springer was our player-coach at the time. His right-hand man, Commander David Dowridge, was playing too. I let a few go and got two or three wickets – not that that was my focus. I wanted to be a batsman.

Anyway, the coach said that, if I ever concentrated on fast bowling, I would be a serious force to be reckoned with. So that's exactly what I tried to do. I was in the gym pumping iron and putting in the hard yards; watching the baseball pitchers and using the biggest ingredient – my heart. A few weeks later I played against St John Culture and bowled so fast. No one wanted to face me. I ended up with four wickets. I'd been bitten by the fast-bowling bug.

When you bowl fast, everyone wants you. At least, everyone wants to be in your team. I was whizzing it down and becoming a sought-after tape-ball star. I played in the Beeland tournament for Garrison School, taking thirty wickets in seven games – the most in the tournament. In three of the games, I took five-fors and ended up being named man of the tournament.

The success kept coming, this time for another team: Ferniehirst. I got the most wickets in the Spooners Hill tournament, which we won, and followed that with the most wickets in the Emerton Lane World Cup for a team called Strugglers. We won that and I was bowling real, real quick. I was nineteen at the time and I must have been bowling that little tape-ball at 99 mph. It was five overs a bowler and mine were sheer speed. I used to bowl everybody, or get them LBW, as I was too quick. Then I'd throw a short one in and hit the batsman in the jaw. I was one of the most feared tape-ball bowlers in Barbados and I knew that, if I could bowl quick with a tape-ball, I could do similar damage with a cricket ball.

With the pace came a bit of cash. I took thirty five wickets in seven games to help Strugglers win the Pine Hill tournament and I took home $1,000. Half was for winning, the other half for ending up as man-of-the-match in the final. Not that I saw a lot of it. It was $500 for mum, $300 for Melissa and $200 for me. I had to take care of the important women in my life. They'd never ask for it but they mattered most, especially with my little lad Tamani less than a year old.

Not everyone was enjoying the speed. I was nineteen when I started to cause a bit of damage. The first victim was a lad called Chissles, a left-handed batter from the neighbourhood who used to come in and bat for ages, holding everyone else up in the process. After all, we all wanted to bat. We were playing tape-ball at the St Leonard's School when I let one go and hit him hard on the temple. The ball left an imprint on his head. Man, that tape-ball hurts. Chissles was in pain. He carried on going but the next bowler knocked his stumps down. When you hit someone, you get them scared – and that's what happened.

Whatever anyone says, batsmen fear fast bowling. They may not all be scared, as such, but they are full of fear. And there's one easy way to tell: the eyes. If you look a batsman in the eye, the eyes never lie. The quick tape-ball bowler from the village – Glenroy Cobin – used to always do it. He told me, 'Tino, look them in the eyes. You can see if they're scared or if they've got big balls.'

I remember bowling at Mahela Jayawardene back in Kandy in 2005. Mahela is a Sri Lankan legend: one of the best batsmen to ever play the game. He played over 650 games in all formats, finishing Test cricket with 11,814 runs at an average of close to 50. He scored another 12,650 runs in ODI cricket. What a player. Now, when I bowled at him that day in Kandy, I could see a scared look in his eyes. I could smell the fear. I bowled one really quick ball at him and he got himself in a bad position. I just looked at him and saw a Sri Lankan great, in front of thousands of home fans who were jamming, in trouble. It doesn't get much better than that.

I knew I could get him. I'd shaken him up and the second ball I bowled at him, in my next over, was pitched up. He hung back and nicked it straight to the late Runako Morton – rest in peace, mate – in the slips. Mahela is class personified. I'm not saying he was scared of the ball, or scared of getting hurt, but quick bowling does weird things to people, even if you're one of the best in the business. His hand was off the bat and his head nowhere near in line. It was so unlike Mahela.

Kumar Sangakkara was up there with Mahela in terms of sheer class. To go up against these batters was an absolute privilege. He once said to me that I was always coming at him. To hear that meant a lot. That's the hallmark of Tino Best: never be afraid and never give up. That's what I learned growing up in the village of Richmond Gap. It only takes one ball to get someone.

Quick bowling doesn't just rough up the batsman facing. If you are bowling well, their team-mates can sense it too. My great friend Devon Malcolm took nine for fifty seven against South Africa and you could see fear crumble their batting line-up. At Yorkshire, in 2010, I was bowling at the speed of sound. I must have been bowling as quick as I had been at any time in my career. But did I get a stack-load of wickets every game? No. I used to get one or two and Steve Patterson – a decent, hard-working seamer who bowled around 80 mph – used to end up with four or five himself. As a pairing, I intimidated and he reaped the rewards. I'm happy with that.

Some batsmen were more susceptible to pace than others. Guys like Freddie Flintoff, Kevin Pietersen and Dilshan would take me on. Lendl Simmons, too, was brilliant. He's the only person in Caribbean first-class cricket to have a go at me consistently. I respect him a lot for that. He has a lot of bottle and will never back down. But there are some batsmen who show a bit more fear than others. You can tell in their expressions.

I especially loved targeting the English. You could be really aggressive and have a go at guys like Marcus Trescothick. He was a good player, Tres, but I thought I always had a chance of just blowing through him. I could be extra aggressive against Mark Butcher and Nasser Hussain too because I knew those two were not going to take me on.

The real shame now? Fast bowlers are a dying breed. The pitches are so flat nowadays and it's killing us. You've got Mitchell Starc and Mitchell Johnson, who can bowl express pace, but they're forced to bowl on flat featherbeds. The only thing you can do is just work so hard at strength and conditioning to make sure you can continue to fire it down. If you don't, your body will break.

I had some real awesome bowling partners: Fidel Edwards, Pedro

Collins, Vasbert Drakes, Kemar Roach, Jason Holder and Jason Bennett, to name a few. These guys were all part of the speed club. They say the key to batting is good partnerships – and that's right. By the same token, the key to good bowling is to bowl in partnerships too. To be a good attack, you have to hunt in packs, just like I did with Steve Patterson at Yorkshire.

For that, my favourite opening bowling partner for Barbados was Ian Bradshaw. Bradshaw and I go way back. Remember, it was him who came off injured in a practice game and gave me a chance to play for Barbados in the first place. I loved Bradshaw. He was just one of the cleverest opening bowlers I'd ever played with. He'd be smart, he'd build the pressure and I knew I could express myself with him. He'd hold a line and length up one end and let me go full throttle and attack at the other. He only played five Tests for the West Indies but I was a massive fan of his. He deserved every one of his sixty two ODI caps.

I loved bowling with Fidel too. For the West Indies, he was my favourite. With Bradshaw, I'd be able to use his ability to hold up an end to exert pressure myself. With Fidel, who played with me for Barbados too, it was just a pure battle of pace. He used to bowl really quick and I'd just want to match him. If he was bowling at 95 mph, I'd want to bowl at 96 mph. He used to inspire me to bowl as quick, if not quicker. We were the same age and just got so charged up bowling together. We'd be like, 'Let's let it fly today,' and that would be really good for me. Nasser Hussain once said we were the quickest bowlers he'd ever faced as a partnership. That was refreshing to hear.

Fidel and I used to be an effective double act. I'll never forget the second Test of our tour to Bangladesh in 2012, in Khulna. Fidel ripped through them in the first innings and took 6 for 90. We piled on the runs after that – Marlon Samuels made 260, Darren Bravo 127 and Shiv Chanderpaul 150 not out – before I took 6 for 40 in the second. We won by ten wickets. That's what Fidel and I could do but, for some reason, we were often separated. It was just one of many selection issues that baffled me.

As for the quickest I've bowled? Well, I bowled some rapid spells in my time: for Yorkshire against Warwickshire, in a T20 in 2010, I was up around 97 mph. I took five for twenty four in a Test match against Bangladesh in 2012, on a flat pitch in Mirpur, bowling real quick but that's what I can do. I've always been all about out-and-out pace. I'll tell young bowlers my pace never dipped and that's because I just loved training and knew I had to be eating the right foods. Brett Lee was the same as me. When I watched him in the Big Bash, he was up at 92 mph in his last game as a thirty-eight-year-old. That's some effort. It shows what you can do if you treat your body right.

Most batsmen gave me a chance and I felt like I could get them out. AB de Villiers smashed 162 not out off 66 balls against the West Indies at the World Cup in Johannesburg in 2015 but even against him I'd back myself to run in, hurt him and get him. He's a genius but I got him twice in one Test. But there are some batsmen that just don't care how quick you're bowling. Rahul Dravid and Hashim Amla are two. What players they are. When bowling at the attacking players, you think you can get them as they'll take you on but Dravid and Amla were something else. You feel you won't get them out if you bowl at them all day.

Brian Lara and Sachin Tendulkar were like that too. On the rare occasion they got hit, they could take pain and they're mentally strong. Those two are legends; geniuses – but Rahul is the best batsman I've ever bowled at. We were playing an ODI in Sri Lanka in 2005 and he hadn't long come to the crease. He came in next and just hit me, easy as you like, for three fours in a row. The first he beat point to his left, then beat point to his right, then he deflected the third past third-man to his right. What a player. Pace didn't scare him.

He gave me one of his shirts after that for my cousin. He told me I had genuine pace and not to sacrifice that for anything. He recognised that I was a quick, quick bowler and that meant so much to me.

As a batsman, I never feared pace because I'd been broken playing tape-ball cricket. I must have had bowlers running up and bowling at 95 mph at my head – no helmet, no pads, nothing. I had Steven Finn bowling at me when I made ninety five batting at eleven in a Test match at Edgbaston. He was trying to take my head off – and why not? He can bowl express pace but I didn't care. I turned round and told him, 'I bowl faster than you and I've hit more people than you.' It made Denesh Ramdin, who was batting at the other end, laugh.

There was a time when there was such thing as a fast-bowlers' union. The bowlers, back in the old days, used never to be able to bat so they'd agree not to bowl bouncers at one another. It was a way of stopping them getting hit, basically. Does that happen now? Not a chance. Fast bowling is a brotherhood off the field but, any time Shaun Tait, Shoaib Ahktar or Brett Lee come into bat, I'm going to pepper them. I'm not going to pitch anything up in their half.

Tait, Akhtar and Lee are going to give it to my batsmen. They're going to try to hurt them. So what are my batsmen going to think if I give the bowlers an easy ride? If I break the opposition quick bowler's finger, he doesn't bowl and he won't hurt my batsmen. Brilliant. When I'm playing for Barbados, Fidel and I are going to pepper the others. If we're off to Jamaica to face Jerome Taylor, we're going to take care of ourselves and give it to him. I bowled a bouncer at Shannon Gabriel once. He's played a few Tests for the West Indies and is real quick. I gave him a bouncer, he fell over and collapsed over his stumps. It was one of the funniest things I've ever seen.

One thing's for sure, fast bowlers have good memories. If you bounce me, I will remember. If it's in the nets, in a club match or in an international match, I know who you are. A few times club bowlers have bowled short balls at me in the nets. I remember them and, when I play them again, they better be able to handle it round their heads, as that's where they're getting it.

Us guys from Barbados love the pace. When we're batting, we'll never fear it. In one game, in March 2005, we were up against Jermaine Lawson, another real quick bowler. He played thirteen Tests for the West Indies and destroyed Australia in a Test match in 2003, taking a hat-trick on his way to seven for seventy eight. He was accused of chucking it when he bowled but, however he got it down, he got it down real quick.

Some of the guys in our dressing room couldn't believe how quick he was bowling but we loved the challenge. He was bowling fast but we wanted him. That's why cricket in Barbados is so good, as we've all got big balls. Gordon Greenidge, Desmond Haynes, the three Ws – Frank Worrell, Clyde Walcott and Everton Weekes – and Carlisle Best, we all loved to hook and cut the short stuff. Barbados is like Western Australia with the bounce of the pitches. It's almost like we'd grown up in Perth. You could dob us some spinners and it had more chance of destroying us than pace.

Sherwin Campbell played 142 times for the West Indies and he loved it short. Philo Wallace played forty and he loved it too. There was one time in 2002 when Ravi Rampaul got Philo out. He chirped him off and Philo was livid, breaking his bat when he came into the training room. 'Next time I see Ravi Rampaul, I'll cut his arse,' he said. 'I'm going to flay him.'

And he did. Ravi was back for more in 2003. Philo had been waiting a year for the chance to play him again and he made a hundred and something. He hit two brand-new balls out the old Kensington Oval and Ravi got so much tap that he was left in tears. Ravi Rampaul was actually crying while Philo was sledging him: 'I'm coming for you, I'm going to chase you off.' We were loving it. That game, Floyd Reifer and Sherwin Campbell made hundreds too and I took four wickets in both innings. That's how us Bajans work. We spend the whole year thinking about things and take a lot of pride in representing our island.

CHAPTER SIX

DOING IT FOR CRASHY

The start of my first first-class season was weeks away. Here I was – Tino la Bertram Best, the champion, the scarily fast bowler – with the chance to fulfil a lifelong dream to play for Barbados. Except the world, the same one I had at my feet, had come crashing down.

Me – and the rest of the Barbados squad – had gone down to the St Ann's Fort for medical tests. I knew it well, given I was part of the BDF Sports Programme and that was where we were based. I was heralded as the pin-up boy when I was there. I'd been the first one to come through the programme to actually make it to professional level, so everyone knew me.

The Barbados squad sat down for lunch with everyone on the base and I took a seat next to my good friend Rondell Pollard – or Crashy, as we knew him. He was a footballer in the sports programme with me and we were part of the same intake in 1998, both younger than most, although Rondell was four months older than me.

I loved him. He was like a footballing-style version of Tino Best. He worked hard and he used to take care of me. If I was in the barracks and I was hungry, he would come and sort me out with crackers and cheese, or a bit of juice. When I was struggling at being dropped from the team, he'd be there to support me. He was inspirational before I was anybody. He believed in me when everyone else didn't.

We sat down to have some lunch that day and he turned to me and said, 'Bamm-Bamm, I want you to work hard. I want you to make it big in cricket. I want you to be an absolute superstar. Don't care what people say – they're going to talk good and bad – just focus on yourself and be a champion. Do you understand what I tell you, Tino?'

Surprised, confused, I agreed: 'Errr, yes, Rondell.' There was more than a hint of hesitancy in my voice so Crashy started again.

'No, Tino. Do you hear what I tell you? You are going to be a star. Put the BDF Sports Programme on the map. You have to do it. You are our man.'

'I'll try, Crashy.'

'No, don't try. Do it. You have to be the one to do it.'

He'd got emotional. These words meant a lot. We hugged. Man, it was chilling. He was living my dream with me. What a man and what a gesture.

The coach for Barbados – and the BDF Sports Programme – at that time was Henderson Springer. He was a real tough cookie with a military background and he was hard as nails. But something wasn't right. A day later I saw him in tears and his watery eyes were red. This wasn't normal. What the hell?

I asked him, 'Coach, what's up?' His answer turned my life upside down.

Rondell was playing football. He was a midfielder – a real good one, who was set to go to Ireland to play. He had dreams to make it big in the Premier League. He was playing a game when he headed the ball and became dazed. Seconds later, he ran, dropped to the floor, collapsed and died. My friend had gone. Rest in peace, Rondell Pollard.

I couldn't believe it. I had to sit down because my knees started to go weak. Crashy's final words were so emotional and now I'd never speak to him again. I cried for two weeks straight. My great friend had died on a football field. I'd seen him every day for four years and now he was gone. That was that. Nothing was ever, ever going to stop me fulfilling my dream. I'd be a star for Barbados, a star for the West Indies, and I was going to make sure I made it for Rondell.

The next week was Crashy's week. I worked my butt off in camp and had his funeral to attend: our final goodbye. It was a military occasion and we were all there in our uniforms. Man, that day was the hardest of my life. There must have been 800 or 900 people there – and every one of them was crying. I sat there thinking of all our chats. We used to shine our boots together and talk through our dreams of becoming superstars together. Now I was at his funeral.

Commander Dowridge and Henderson Springer were both there: two strong men, emotional as anyone. I turned and said, 'Coach and Sir, I will make it for Crashy. I will put the BDF Sports Programme on the map.' Dowridge turned and told me, 'You don't have a choice, Tino. You have to.'

Our first game of the season for Barbados was on 25 January 2002 against Guyana. Most players in the Caribbean get their chance aged twenty three or twenty four. It's not like England, where players tend to break into their county sides earlier. But here I was, twenty years old, with the chance of a lifetime. Wow.

Just as Uncle Carlisle had told me, the hard work was to start now. I'd made the squad – great – but it wouldn't mean a thing if I didn't play. And how could I let Rondell down? I couldn't.

I knew how to impress Henderson, who was a hard taskmaster.

Henderson beasted people in training and I knew what he expected of his players. 'Hard work will always beat talent that doesn't work hard,' he used to say. Springs had been in the Barbados job for a year and demanded a lot of his players. I'd work around the clock to be the best and the fittest, I thought. That was my plan. That's how I'd fulfil Rondell's dreams.

The Barbados squad that I was coming into was full of stars. There was Courtney Browne, Floyd Reifer, Sherwin Campbell, Ryan Hinds and Philo Wallace, for a start. All those played for the West Indies. Then there was Ian Bradshaw, who played for the Windies too. As for me, with Pedro Collins and Corey Collymore away with the West Indies on a tour to Pakistan, I'd be battling Fidel Edwards and Antonio Thomas for two out of three fast-bowling places.

All three of us were quick with the ability to bowl at over 90 mph. Fidel, like me, hadn't been around the youth teams but Antonio had. Everyone thought very highly of him. He'd played for the Under-15s and the Under-19s and was ahead of us in the pecking order. So, if he got one spot, it was me versus my great mate Fidel for the other.

Thanks to my uncle, I already knew a few of the players. When he played for Barbados, he used to take me into the dressing room as a young boy, where I'd get the chance to pick their brains. Some of those same guys were still around. Except I'd gone from the chatty kid who watched to the chatty kid who played. I was now their team-mate.

The likes of Floyd and Courtney were like brothers to me from the moment I walked into the set-up. Those two were – and still are – two of my best friends in cricket. I stuck to Courtney a lot in camp. He was one of the guys who knew me from my days with Uncle Carlisle. In fact, he used to dish out chewing gum to me when I was a kid. And no, not because my breath smelt. It was his plan to shut me up.

From the moment I arrived, I told him how much I wanted to get in the final XI. I'd never played a first-class game or been in the Barbados environment so Courtney kept me focused and told me what to do. I was the little bro. He protected me and I owe him a lot for that.

Floyd and I were sleeping next to each other in camp one night when I talked to him about similar things. These guys played for the West Indies, they were in their prime but here they were in bunk beds in army facilities. It must have been hard for them. They would have been used to nice hotels with comfy beds but they loved it.

Floyd told me, 'Tino, you must be fitter and stronger than the other fast bowlers – then you'll make it.' So that's exactly what I set out to do. I'd run bleep tests to level seventeen. I'd bowl longer spells than the other fast bowlers in practices, to get ahead of them and to keep my body fit and my mind fresh. If the captain turned to me when I was tired in a game, I could still do the job. I wanted to do what the other bowlers couldn't.

Barbados has had such a rich history. We've won twenty four-day championships. No one in first-class cricket anywhere in the world can match our success at domestic level. There was so much of a legacy, so many years of success, and now I could be a part of it.

I was working my butt off. I needed to get into the side – it was do or die. The elder guys were impressed as I tuned my mind to beat everyone in training. They loved the energy. Not everyone did though. I think it made some of the younger guys a bit annoyed. I think they thought, 'Oh, wow, he's just trying to impress the coach' – and so what? I was. I don't think there was animosity, as such. I don't think I was hated. I just knew I had to do whatever it took to make it.

Coach Springer is a man who wants to win everything. He'd told me to work hard, put in the effort and that I'd get somewhere at the BDF Sports Programme. And I had. Now I'd been called up to the

Barbados squad and that philosophy wasn't going to change. I knew I wasn't as talented as the others but I knew I could grind and be stronger than them.

After days of graft – bowling, sprinting and lifting weights – I was ready. It was the night before the game against Guyana when the team was announced. With Sherwin away with the West Indies, Philo was our captain and he began to read the names out. Antonio was selected. He'd made it. There was one more spot left. It was Fidel or me for the other place.

Philo paused, then, after what seemed like an age, said, 'Tino Best.' YES! I was in. The dream was reality. I'd walk out at the Kensington Oval a Barbados player. That one's for you, Crashy boy.

I thought it was a dream when I woke up the next day. My mum always used to make me a big breakfast when I had cricket and this was no different – even if I'd be playing for Barbados now and not some tape-ball game. The smell of eggs, bacon and toast filled the house and I got it down me and off I went. My mum is just such a champion. It was just like any other day. It all felt so natural.

We batted first and Philo Wallace and Kurt Wilkinson were going well. They took us to 189 for 1 but then we collapsed to 304 all out. If it wasn't for Courtney Browne, who made fifty two, it could have been even worse. I only made four – not that I was that nervous. I wanted to be a batsman as a kid but I was in for my bowling. I went out and tried to hit a few shots off leg-spinner Mahendra Nagamootoo, who played a few games for the West Indies, before Neil McGarrell got me out caught. I just wanted to entertain the crowd.

Everyone was preparing to leave the ground that day when the announcer put out a message on the public address system that there'd be two overs left to be bowled. I'd have my chance to show the world what I could do.

I marked my run-up out and stood and looked around the Kensington Oval. What a ground; what a place. There were so many emotions. There must have been 4,000 people in there. It filled up as the day went on, people coming in after work. I looked up towards my mum and aunt in the stands. Man, they looked so excited. Mum was shouting, 'Come on Tino. You can do it.' Dad wasn't there – of course he wasn't there – but Mum's excitement was enough for two.

I took off my cap and gave it to umpire Steve Bucknor. His reaction? He laughed: 'Why are you opening the bowling? You're as small as ever!' Yeah, all right, Steve. You just wait. He didn't know what was coming. I told him I bowled fast. 'Let's see it then,' he replied.

I got to my mark and took a deep breath. All I could think about was Rondell – Crashy, my best mate. I wish he was here to see it. I looked up to the heavens and spoke: 'Crashy, please calm me, bro. This is for you.'

Azeemul Haniff, who took the strike, and Sewnarine Chattergoon were the two openers. I stormed in, let it go and, man, it must have been the fastest ball I'd ever bowled. It nearly took Haniff's head off. Courtney leaped up and caught the ball high above his head. As for Haniff: he was on the ground. It didn't hit him but it put him on his backside.

I turned and saw umpire Bucknor.

'Who are you? Oh my God, who are you again?' he said.

'Tino Best.'

'My gosh, boy, you've got some serious wheels.'

I could feel the buzz of the place. The crowd were getting behind me – the local boy on his debut.

The second ball was outside off stump and Haniff was nowhere near in line. He didn't fancy it. The third ball was a short, lifting delivery and he got out the way this time. At least he stayed on his feet. I was building up a head of steam and I was loving every minute of it. The fourth ball was full, fast and it beat him again. Had he forgotten his bat?

The slip cordon was pumping me up. 'Yes, Animal.' 'Come on baby Akhtar.' 'Come on baby Brett Lee.' They were buzzing for me.

I let go of the fifth ball of the over – a short, lifting, throat-cutter. Haniff edged it and it flew to Floyd Reifer. It went fast and it went high but Floyd must be 6 foot, 3 or 4 inches. There he was – my big-brother figure – to take the catch.

A Haniff. Ct Reifer b Best. 0

I couldn't believe it. I went mental. I ran straight towards the players' pavilion and the Kensington Oval was going wild. There was my auntie and mum, screaming at the tops of their voices. That one's for you, Crash. That one's for you.

The final ball of the over to Travis Dowlin was fast. How it didn't bowl him, I don't know. Ian Bradshaw then ran in and bowled a maiden, line and length – medium pace, typical Bradshaw. They were one down at the close. What a start.

I took a deep breath and took it all in. The small boy from Richmond Gap was performing on the big stage. I looked towards my mum and auntie in the Kensington stand, with the sun going down behind it, and waved. There they were, as proud as punch, clapping away with the biggest grins in Barbados. Philo told me to lead the team off so I did, smiling away with a host of Barbados legends behind me.

In the dressing room, I paused again. The emotion had become overwhelming. I sat and stopped to think about Rondell. He'd told me to put the BDF Sports Programme on the map. I must fulfil his wish.

Then I thought of the programme itself, of all the sportsmen there, the hours they graft, of Commander Dowridge. These people put so much into it. I just wanted to give something back to them.

And my family. I felt all the positive energy from them and how much they'd supported me. People had beaten me down my whole life and told me I wouldn't make it. But tell me I'm not going to do something and I'll work twice as hard to do it. This was the first step on the ladder.

Then my mind wandered on to my father. I could feel all the emotion of him not being there – not that I let it bother me. The only effect it would have was a positive one. I'd channel the pain and the hurt in the most positive of ways. God knows where he was that day. I wouldn't have any idea. I'd done it all for Rondell, for Mum, for Coach Springer and for Commander Dowridge – not for him.

The next day I revved up and let go more of the same. I yorked Dowlin and had him plum LBW, beaten for pace, in the first over of the day. He'd go on to play six Tests for the West Indies but I was just too quick. Tino la Bertram Best had a second victim.

Chattergoon was next, nicking one behind to Courtney Browne. The evening before, he'd walked off and told me that day two would be serious – it was. I'd got rid of the top three, all for ducks, two of the catches taken by my best buddies.

Our momentum was stalled by Andre Percival, a real seasoned player coming in at six. He never made the Test or one-day teams for the West Indies but he could play. In between overs he told me I was the quickest thing he had ever faced, which meant a lot. Percival made 96 that day and brought Guyana up to 231, still 73 behind but it gave them a chance. I got their skipper, Nagamootoo, for a duck – the fourth batsman I'd got without scoring – and ended up with four for fifty from fifteen overs.

I could have had a fifth wicket too. I got one of their tail-enders out, caught at short leg but I overstepped and it was a no-ball. Not that I cared. I wasn't that bothered on missing out on milestones as I was living the dream. I'd come from the St Leonard's School, where I'd grown up wanting to be a batsman, and had just taken four wickets on debut. I had proved I had what it takes to compete. Sometimes it's not about talent, it's about balls, and I had them. I spent hours lifting weights, running round fields, lifting more weights and running round more fields. All the hard work had paid off.

All the batsmen chipped in during the second innings and I even had a chance to come in and smash a couple of fours in my twelve not out. It was like tape-ball all over again! We declared with a lead of 401 before skittling them out for 239 to win the first game of the season. I didn't take a wicket in the second innings but our spinner, Ryan Austin, did the hard work by taking five. Coach Springer was a happy man.

So my first game was done, we'd won and I'd banked my first Barbados pay cheque. I felt blessed – not that the money would get me far. I wasn't driven by the cash but I'll tell you now: first-class cricketers in the West Indies are not well paid. I got paid $195 for playing a first-class match, which is about £125 in English money. So we're talking $50 or £30 for each day I played. The West Indian players, like Sherwin Campbell, got $650. Put simply, you have to play for the West Indies if you want to make anything in cricket. Fortunately, I was living between my gran and Mum's houses at the time with no real outgoings, except bits for Tamani and money for Melissa, so I didn't desperately need the dollar.

If the first game was the dream debut, my second game was a rude awakening. Windward Islands were next to play us at the Kensington Oval and they beat us for the first time in something like thirty years. Personally, I didn't bowl too badly. I was expensive but took a couple of wickets in the first innings to record figures of thirteen overs, two for sixty five. The second was easily forgotten: six overs, no wicket, thirty six runs conceded.

The opening day was the first time I came up against a batsman by the name of Devon Smith. He was a class act, making 143 before Sulieman Benn had him LBW. He absolutely creamed it that day and I remember thinking, 'Man, this guy is good. First-class cricket is real serious stuff'. Devon played thirty eight Tests for the West Indies and scored just the one hundred, against England at Sabina Park in 2004. He ended with a Test average of twenty four and a half but he was a far better player than that. Even then, I knew he was quality. I knew he'd be a competitor I'd love to play against throughout my career.

We were soon up to Jamaica for my first away game. I hadn't ever played cricket outside Barbados. And, more still, I hadn't been on a plane since I was nine. We were staying at the Four Seasons hotel – a real nice place, with different food and a different culture. My first room-mate was Courtney Browne – surprise, surprise – who was brilliant. He took me under his wing and talked to me about cricket and life. Anything from girls to bowling bouncers to property investments, Courtney was my man.

He told me that here, in Jamaica, was the real place I had to impress. Jamaicans loved fast bowling and I knew that, if I wanted to be big in West Indies cricket, I'd have to do well at Sabina Park.

I'd taken six wickets in my opening two games – a decent start but not sensational – yet all the talk was about me before the game. Philo spoke in his press conference about how quick I was, bigging me up and telling everyone I was a real talent.

Except it was Jamaica's Daren Powell who did the damage on the first day. He didn't have the express pace that I did but he was sharpish and skilful with a good action. The West Indies selectors knew that and he played thirty seven Tests for us although, with an average of forty eight, he didn't pull up any trees. Daren went through our top order and he got the number eleven too – me – to end with figures of five for twenty eight.

Desperate to show what I could do, I cranked up the pace. I steamed in, bowled real quick and the fans loved it. The Jamaicans were chanting my name in Sabina Park. What the heck? I was playing AGAINST them. I was even hitting their batsmen but they were loving it. It was electrifying; incredible. They'd tell me to bowl with more fire and to wind it up even more. They were so enthralled that I was so small yet bowling so quickly. I took four for seventy five off my twenty overs but we collapsed and lost by an innings and thirty nine runs.

After the game, Jamaica's all-rounder, Laurie Williams, found me in the hotel while I was chilling by the pool. He told me I had real pace, determination and said how much he loved seeing a West Indian bowler who wanted to keep running in. He was an experienced pro and I enjoyed hearing his words. He encouraged me, Fidel and Antonio to keep going. His words will always stay with me.

Sadly, later that year – 2002 – Laurie passed away when his car hit a bus. Rest in peace, Laurie Williams. Never forgotten. He'd joined my mate Crashy in heaven. Two tragedies and two men who I'll never forget, gone in the space of less than twelve months. Life can be cruel.

After the good start, we'd lost two in a row. Captain Philo was pissed off but he didn't stop encouraging me. I was beating myself up. Two losses? Damn, I must do better. I told myself I needed to work harder, to take more wickets with the new ball and start doing some damage up front.

We headed to Trinidad and word among everyone was how quick I was bowling. If there was a quickie around, news of it spread like wildfire. They'd heard of a short bloke bowling so quick that they should be worried. You see, talk in those days was like Chinese whispers. There were no speed guns and no TV-highlights packages to see. They'd hear of a little kid called Tino Best: a short lad bowling with the pace of Shoaib Akhtar. That just didn't happen. Batsmen were scared.

Two young players made their debuts for Trinidad on 15 February 2002. One was named Dwayne Bravo, the other Ravi Rampaul. Those two were my enemies on the field but they'd turn into team-mates one day. We would go on to play more than 400 games for the West Indies between us. It was brilliant playing against them. They, like me, were considered the best young players around.

I ran in, bowled rapid on a flat wicket and the Trinidadians didn't want it. I would have killed them on a quicker track. I huffed and puffed but the canny Ravi fared better. Their bowlers just knew how to bowl on the Queen's Park Oval wicket. Ravi wasn't quick but he was so clever, even at the age of just seventeen, taking four wickets in the first innings. It was more misery for us and we lost by four wickets. I took two for fifty four in the first innings and none for forty two in the second. Their camp was delighted. We'd lost three in a row and it was then, seeing all the Trinidad faces, that I realised how real and serious the rivalry in the inter-islands competition was.

We left Trinidad, and the West Indies boys – who had been away touring Pakistan – arrived back with us. Sherwin Campbell, Pedro Collins and Corey Collymore were all recalled to the side – rightly so, they were our best players – which meant I was out. I had taken two four-fors in my twelve wickets but I could have had more. I had a lot of drops off my bowling.

Bangladesh A played in our tournament as part of their development and we got back to our winning ways against them, largely thanks to Sherwin Campbell hitting a hundred and Collymore and Collins getting five-wicket hauls. I was then left out again as we drew with the Leeward Islands.

With Jamaica well on course to win the Busta Cup, the last game of the season meant nothing. We were due to play the West Indies B – a university side who played in the competition for four years in the early 2000s – at the Kensington Oval. Courtney, sensing I should play and playing his big-brother role again, had a few words with Sherwin.

'You've got to play Tino. He's the quickest bowler in the Caribbean. You can't let him sit on the bench,' he said. And with that, I was back.

Sherwin, Kurt Wilkinson and Ryan Hinds all made hundreds as we racked up 557 for 7 before we declared. I had six wicketless overs in their reply as Collins and Collymore took the new ball and, thanks to Sulieman Benn's five-for, West Indies B were soon following on.

I had one final chance; one innings left of the season to make an impact. I had to make this count.

So I did what I do. I steamed in, gave it my all and blasted away five of the top six. Three out LBW, one caught behind and one caught and bowled. We ripped West Indies B out for 101. I walked off the pitch, having taken five for thirty seven, close to tears. Courtney was as proud as punch. He held me tight, beaming from ear to ear. The papers were writing about me and, most importantly, mum was smiling.

My first first-class five-wicket haul was followed by a West Indies A call-up to tour England. That's the BDF Sports Programme on the map for you, Crashy. God bless you, mate. I loved him – everyone loved him. I will forever remember sitting in the chapel at his funeral as the hardest day of my life. He'd gone but I made sure I kept on fighting. I had no choice but to make it in cricket. May Rondell continue to rest in peace to this day.

CHAPTER SEVEN

THE PLAYBOY LIFESTYLE

I love girls – and girls love me. I reckon I'm the best-looking bald-headed guy in the world. I joke about being the black Brad Pitt!

Everywhere I went as a cricketer, I'd talk to girls, date girls and sleep with girls. I reckon I've slept with anywhere between 500 and 650 girls, all around the world.

I can bowl at 90 mph and I'm confident. The result is that plenty of women are always interested. Now don't get me wrong: I loved Melissa. I cheated on her and it was a huge mistake. A massive mistake – one of the biggest mistakes of my life. I'm the first to admit that. I tried to win Melissa back and it failed. She was the mother of my beautiful child but she wasn't interested. Fair enough. The lads had told me that, once I took wickets for Barbados, she'd come running back for me. I had done just that but she hadn't. When she called it a day, I became a bit of a playboy. Put it this way: I was a man whore.

If I liked a girl, I'd go and talk to them – whoever it was. If I'd seen

Beyoncé and she was single, I'd have gone and introduced myself: 'Hello, my name's Tino. What's yours?' No girl intimidated me.

I met a lot of girls at a place called The Boatyard in Barbados. I used to chill there with Courtney Browne, Sulieman Benn, Floyd Reifer and Sherwin Campbell. It had a real cool vibe. It wasn't a nightclub, more a beach bar where you could have a drink, lounge and meet different people.

I was younger than the rest of my team-mates when I first arrived on the scene. I was handsome and single and girls liked that. They liked the fact there was no strings attached with me too.

I was desperate to impress the older lads when I got in the Barbados squad because we had a brotherhood together. I was the new kid on the block and I felt like I'd get points from the boys when I pulled a girl. It was a way of getting more respect and showing I was the man.

The Barbados and West Indies lads used to like a drink but there was no huge drinking culture. They never encouraged me to drink, put it that way, and I never felt pressurised. It was more of a social drink – one or two brandies – and it wouldn't end up out on the piss. I used to train so hard that I couldn't afford to fill myself with booze and throw that down the drain. Risk the opportunity of playing for the West Indies? No chance, bro.

I'd pick and choose who I wanted to date. I used to go on five or six dates a week, all with different girls. So, yes, I was a man whore. I'd have to juggle them round. One on one day, another on another day. I was young and loving the lifestyle.

My mum said she didn't mind me having lots of girls – if I was careful. And there's one thing I never did – I'd never lie to a girl. I'd always tell them straight: I don't want a relationship and all I'm interested in is having fun. No relationship, no stress. It was one bit of advice Floyd always used to tell me. You don't have to tell girls lies. Just be honest.

Once Melissa left, I didn't like the thought of having to answer to someone. I didn't want to be steaming in for Barbados against Jamaica at Sabina Park, worrying if my wife or girlfriend was back home cheating while I was away. I have my whole life to find someone – cricket is a short career.

All the girls knew the score. They knew I was a travelling athlete and they knew I wasn't husband material. Marriage is not really encouraged in our society anyway. People tend to break up so much. You'll spend a load of money building a million-dollar house, split up and the other half will want to have half the damn house. I always wanted to wait and, even then, it has to be the right girl. I'm not going to rush it.

We used to go on tour with the West Indies – and away with Barbados – and see how many girls we could enjoy. If I went to Australia and saw a nice-looking blonde, I'd want to date them. If I went to South Africa and saw a gorgeous brunette, I'd want to go out for a bit with her. I always used to tease my team-mates and tell them that, if they didn't play cricket, they wouldn't get the girls. I'd get girls because I'm good looking, I'd joke!

We used to have competitions of who could shag the most girls on tour. My record, on an eleven-week tour to Australia in 2005, was over forty. I was twenty four and I didn't play a Test on that tour. The coach, Bennett King, didn't fancy me one bit. He must have been the only one who didn't! He made me watch the Test matches and I used to feel so frustrated. All I did was play the tour games.

But I was bowling fast – at night. I'd go out partying on my own, pick up a girl and take her back to the hotel. I wasn't out drinking much on those nights. I'd have a brandy but I would train and work so hard, so I didn't want much alcohol. I knew drinking would undo all the hard work I was putting in. I'd always be fitter, faster and stronger than everyone else. Nothing would get in the way of that. I wanted girls – not alcohol.

I'd go out, pick up a couple of girls and take them back to our hotel. A plush hotel with a professional sportsman: the girls loved it. Sometimes I'd take back four girls on one night! If that happened, I'd have to call one of the other lads for back-up to help me out.

I've had plenty of threesomes, or *ménages à trois*, as I like to call them. One night I had three girls at once. That's the most I've ever done stuff with. I wasn't getting any play on the field in Australia – but I was at night.

The greatest night of my life was in 2004. I had my first *ménage à trois* in the Crowne Plaza hotel in Birmingham. Wow. I went for dinner with two beautiful girls and took them back to my room. That blew my mind.

The most beautiful girls are the Australians. I think they are amazing. They are really into their fitness and have amazing bodies.

Did any of this affect my cricket? No, not at all. I don't think it hindered me. There was no one who trained harder than me for Barbados or the West Indies. If I bring two girls back and have sex with them, I'll still be out there first in the morning working hard. I was smart about it and didn't get into any trouble. I respected that I played for my country and did everything I could – but I liked enjoying myself too.

I'd take girls back to hotel rooms but no one would know. I'd still train my butt off and I wasn't flaunting it about. I'd move and walk about so slyly. In 2005 I told our coach, Bennett King, that I was heavily committed to my girlfriend back in Barbados – but I didn't even have one! He'd seen me out with a few girls in Adelaide and I needed an excuse.

I go after girls I want – and I don't talk to groupies. I don't want girls coming up and saying they know me through cricket. I go after them – not the other way round.

People used to know me in Barbados but it was different abroad. A lot of girls recognised me and said I was familiar but they thought I was an American who played American Football or something. That suited me. I didn't tell them I played cricket for the West Indies. They just knew I was a professional sportsman and thought I must have been on vacation.

It's a different ball game with girls now, what with social media being so big. Back when I started, in 2002, I could do as I liked without the threat of everyone knowing all my business. I was so quiet about what I did and used to go under the radar. Nowadays, it's different. People have camera phones, Facebook and Twitter. Now everyone can know your business.

People text and use Whatsapp and everything can be screen-shotted. Then they can be posted online or sent to other people and everyone knows everything. I prefer to call people, rather than text. As for sending naughty pictures, no way. I'm too smart for that!

There was a news story that came out in September 2015 when Chris Gayle went on Instagram to post about his strip club. He put up a picture and wrote, 'From the pool to the strip club…if u don't have a strip club at home, U ain't a cricket 'Player' .. I always make sure my guest well entertained and feel like they are at home #LifeIsForLiving #DreamBig.'

Now, Chris is good fun but he doesn't indulge in too much bad stuff. He's a good man, Chris. The most fun on a night out is Dwayne Bravo. We complemented each other very well when we played for the West Indies together. I'll give him an award now: he's the best wingman going!

Don't get me wrong, I respect girls very much. I come from a family of strong women but in the Caribbean things are just more laid back and it's what people do. No one was getting hurt, no one was being led on and everyone knew where they stood.

If Melissa had taken me back, I'd have been much cooler and things would have been different but it wasn't to be. I've slept with plenty of women while she's settled down and had another baby. Fair play to her. I hope everything goes perfectly for Melissa. She's a special woman.

The girls might have liked me a lot but some of the guys didn't. Courtney Browne once told me to expect the fact that guys wouldn't take to me because I was young, could bowl fast and I was good looking and confident. I could always carry a conversation too. The girls loved it, the blokes didn't. There's always a tinge of jealousy from other men when they see you talking to girls.

The girls are great but the best thing about being a cricketer is the days on the field. Nothing can beat pulling on the whites of your country and going into battle. It's a feeling like no other. Some people ask me the worst thing about being a cricketer and, you know what? There isn't a single thing I don't enjoy.

You are travelling a lot, living in hotel rooms, moving from place to place but I don't hate it, not one bit. I'm the total opposite: I love it. There aren't many jobs in the world where you get paid so well for doing something you love. With it, you're travelling the world too. India, Sri Lanka, Bangladesh, England, Australia… the list goes on. I've had the chance to go to cities in all these countries. I'll never ever take that for granted.

Tours weren't easy but they'd be really enjoyable. I like having the chance to bond even tighter as a group and getting to know all the lads. The boys will train hard and then, as we're all together, we'll go and spend plenty of time talking and chatting even more. If we have a day off, we'll go and explore the town or the country we're in.

I loved everywhere we went. Queenstown, in New Zealand, is a really nice town, really pretty. I went out there with Virgil Browne, who was our masseur with the West Indies. He's a fantastic human being. I'm really close with Virgil and we had a great time in Queenstown. It's a bit cold but there's just so much to see.

I used to love the formal events we had to go to as well. I loved going to the Prime Minister's residence in Canberra, Australia, and getting the chance to have a glass of wine and mix with diplomats throughout the world. We went and saw the High Commissioner in India – what a part of the world to go to. Every time I pulled on that blazer, I was on a high. It made me reflect on what I'd achieved and how much of an honour it was to represent my country.

But I'm sorry to anyone who lives in Khulna: I can't say the same for that city. It's the third largest in Bangladesh and houses the Sheikh Abu Naser Stadium. It became the country's seventh Test cricket venue on 21 November 2012, when we played Bangladesh. I have so many happy memories from that game. I took six for forty – my best ever figures in Test cricket – in the second innings. I got three of the top four out and we won the game by ten wickets. Happy days.

Except it's not all great memories. Most cities I used to familiarise myself with but not Khulna. In fact, it's probably one of the only places in the whole world I didn't go out and explore. Put it this way: it's not Melbourne. The two places are like chalk and cheese. I love Bangladesh and the people are great – very passionate – but I just found Khulna quite rough and didn't feel at home. I didn't get out much at all while I was there. I just stayed in my hotel room and watched Netflix most of the time. The hotel was clean, which is the most important thing. The beds were OK too but it's just not the Royal Kensington Hotel in London, is it? You can't compare the two.

I got a deal to play for Sylhet Royals in the Bangladesh Premier League in 2013 but I never went out there. It was worth a nice sum of money but the West Indies called me up instead. I was a bit relieved, to be honest, as Bangladesh wasn't my favourite place in the world to go. That or the chance to play for my country again? You know where I'd rather be.

It wasn't just me who didn't fancy getting out and about in Bangladesh. Most of the guys stayed in their rooms. One thing about Bangladesh is – and Sri Lanka is the same – they have curfews. There are some laws saying you're not supposed to be out and about on the road past midnight – at least, that's what they told me.

That rule caught me out once. We were in Kandy in Sri Lanka for a Test in 2005 when I met a girl who worked for the United Nations. She was a nice girl so I went and sat and had a few drinks with her. It got to the time when I was about to leave and she stopped me: 'You can't leave now.' I had to ask her why and she said there was a curfew.

So I had to go, sleep in her room then get a tuk tuk back to the hotel the next day! It was only a fifteen-minute trip but thank God we didn't have a Test match the day after.

Going out in the different cities and getting to see what's about takes your mind away from the cricket. It's important to do that, as it can just become too much. Cricket, twenty four hours a day, seven days a week – it can be tough. In a big city, I'd go out to the movies and walk around. Not in Bangladesh. What got me through the tour in 2012 was *Family Guy*. Most people will know what it is but, if you don't, it's an American adult-animated sitcom – and it's hilarious. I got through series one to series ten when I was out there. I preferred to stay in and watch DVDs than be out and about. It made the time go quicker.

We're lucky with food nowadays in that all the big cities tend to cater for all the different nationalities. It is probably far, far easier for my generation than it was in the past, as restaurants cater for more international people.

I love England because I can get my Caribbean food and it feels like home. I like my sweet potatoes and grilled fish and England is great for that. Australia and New Zealand are good but you've got to eat what they're eating, generally. They do good chicken but it's not prepared how we have it in the Caribbean. It's not too bad but, outside the West Indies, England is the best for the food.

I wouldn't have gone to half the places I've gone to without cricket. I'm always grateful that I've had chances to get away and I found we'd always come back stronger as a squad after a tour. Some international cricketers have struggled being away. Take Marcus Trescothick and Jonathan Trott, for example. They were two great batsmen but both had issues with being away from England and away from their family.

Fortunately for me, I didn't have issues like that to deal with. I was always single, of course, and I didn't have any worries about being away from a partner. It was tough to be away from Tamani for long periods but I'd spend time with him when I was back. When I wasn't playing cricket I loved taking care of him. We'd have weeks together, just me and him, and we always had a very good bond. I just used to love holding him, hugging him and kissing him. I used to let him sleep next to me. He is my everything.

The BDF Sports Programme helped me massively in terms of coping with life on the road. You get used to being alone in the army scheme and that's what helped when it came to spending long periods away from loved ones playing cricket. I was never bored in the hotels or on flights as I had the other lads for company.

Team meetings were never dull either. Some players may not like them but, with the West Indies, they were always good fun. We'd be serious but I'd enjoy it. It all came down to the spirit in the camp. There was a good bond off the field and we'd always be cracking jokes. A lot of credit should go to Richie Richardson and Ottis Gibson for the spirit they got going in the camp in my latter days in the set-up. We'd play dominoes for hours with each other and they ensured it was a nice environment to be in.

If we weren't playing dominoes, we'd be playing cards or video games. It's like we were our very own family. We bonded well and there was never really any beef. We wouldn't argue over girls or anything like that and, although sometimes we might get a little heated with each other, it'd never get serious. People like to say crap about us fighting each other or having disagreements. No. The West

Indies team was never like that when I was in it. At times it was lonely but we respected each other too much to fight.

Another perk of the job is how we travelled. We'd be flying business or upper class everywhere. I've never been on a private jet but the Virgin and British Airways ones were great. I would spend hours reading spy books, which brought me back to my childhood. My grandmother never gave me many toys to play with. Instead, she'd give me Enid Blyton books to read and I'd sit and get through them. I felt like a kid again on those planes.

Most of the other guys would just relax, sleep or watch movies. We were all from the small Caribbean islands and we'd be travelling to a big city like Melbourne. That was a great experience for all of us and you'd never know when you could be on your last tour. You had to savour every minute. The travel was all sorted out by our team managers: Ricky Skerritt and Tony Howard were two of the best. They'd organise all the flights and always make sure the guys were nice and comfortable.

I was friends with pretty much everyone in the West Indies camp. Darren Sammy and I were very cool and he was one of my closest mates. Narsingh Deonarine and I were good friends too. We played a lot against each other and I always enjoyed his company. He's a couple of years younger than me and will always be the last man to get out Sachin Tendulkar in a Test match. In fact, it was Darren and Narsingh who combined for that one. Tendulkar was caught Sammy bowled Deonarine for seventy four in Mumbai in 2013. Not a bad wicket to get.

Adam Sanford was a little bit older than me but we were always close. Wavell Hinds may have dropped a few catches in the slips off my bowling but he was tremendous to me. Wavell's another brilliant human being, as is Ridley Jacobs. I'm not sure if he liked me much though. He was our wicket-keeper and he always had ice on his hands because I'd been bruising them through bowling so fast!

Although I didn't get on with everybody. There was one player, who I respect very much as a cricketer, who had a bit of a problem with me. We just never gelled as we should have. When I first joined the West Indies team in 2003, he came and visited me and wanted a West Indies sweater. He hadn't made it by that point. I didn't give it to him and handed over a couple of pairs of Adidas spikes instead. I really loved him as a man but I didn't want to give away the stuff I'd earned. Uncle Carlisle taught me that. I wanted him to earn his West Indies sweater, like I had to.

He went on to do just that and played many times for the West Indies – and I'm so glad he did. He had the hunger and desire to do well. I only found out ten years later how much that incident had hurt him. He felt I'd been stingy and it really, really got to him. We don't talk now – all over a jersey. He's achieved a lot and I'm genuinely, genuinely happy he has. Good on him for that but different things clearly affect different people. I still feel I was in the right. You have to earn your West Indies stripes.

CHAPTER EIGHT

TESTING TIMES

'Tino, the phone's for you!' Mum shouted.

It was a normal April day in 2003. I was at my mum's in St James's, having watched the West Indies lose the first Test against the Aussies in Guyana. The first-class season had finished and I was relaxing. I'd had a real good second season but this was chill time. The phone ringing had disturbed a bit of quiet. I got off the sofa to pick it up.

'Tino, it's Stephen Alleyne, the president of the Barbados Cricket Board.'

Woah. 'Hi, good afternoon,' I just about managed to reply.

He had news for me. It wasn't the West Indies, was it? Was this really happening? Was it a prank? I could hear a sense of pride in his voice as he started again: so formally, so sincerely, so professionally.

'It gives me the biggest joy to give you the news that you've been selected in the squad for the second Test in Trinidad.'

What. The. Frig. I couldn't believe my ears. I stopped him, muzzled the phone and let out the biggest scream. YESSSSSSSSSSSSSS!

Mr Alleyne continued, 'Your great Uncle Carlisle will be so proud for you to follow in his footsteps. I wish you the best for an illustrious career. My advice for you: play the same way for the West Indies as you do for Barbados – and the flight leaves tomorrow. See you at the airport.'

Brian Lara, the captain, had hinted it might happen. I was coming off the back of a real good year and had made a name for myself – and it was all down to Courtney Browne. In December 2002 he had been made captain. He'd done the job before and led Barbados to the four-day title back in 1995 – only to lose the captaincy a year later. But six years on he was back and, crucially for me, he was my best friend in cricket.

Springer and Browne proved a mightily effective combination. Courtney had so much faith in me. He told me before the season that I had to get the most wickets that year and he set me a target of forty. If I got that, he said, we'd win the cup.

When Courtney says something, you just believe it. The man has that aura about him. I knew it could be a breakthrough year but the way he used me was just incredible. It was – and still is – the best I'd ever been captained. He used to bowl me three or four overs up front with the new ball. I'd go full throttle, give it everything and bowl as fast as I could. I might get one wicket for twenty runs and then he'd take me off and bring Ian Bradshaw on to shore things up and assert some control.

Then, at eighty for three or four, I'd come back on and tend to get a couple more out before returning to clean up the tail. In nine games I took thirty nine wickets at an average of twenty. I won the Courtney Walsh award for the most wickets in a season as we topped the table and won the Carib Beer Cup. We'd gone from having a shit season to becoming champions: Barbados's eighteenth four-day crown and my first. Tino la Bertram Best was a champion.

In that same year I got Lara out at the Kensington Oval, nicked off to Courtney Browne. Unsurprisingly, he was the most memorable scalp of the thirty nine. When Courtney Walsh presented me with the award, it was one of the best moments of my life. I dedicated it to Rondell and his father called me up to thank me. He needn't have. Rondell is always, always in my thoughts.

Jermaine Lawson had been with the West Indies but he had symptoms of chickenpox and the selectors, seeing I was one for the future, wanted me in as cover. I thanked Mr Alleyne, hung up the phone and set about telling everyone. And I mean everyone. My mum, my brother, my sisters, the neighbours, the kids outside, the guys who worked in the mini-mart in the neighbourhood. Everyone. They were high-fiving and mum was crying. I hugged her so tightly. These were tears of joy, tears of pride. She had me so young and she'd been through so much. Some young men at twenty or twenty one are getting into trouble or making bad decisions but she'd brought me up to become an international cricketer. Her first-born child had been called up to play for the West Indies. I nearly cried myself I was so happy for her. I was so happy to be her son.

I called Uncle Carlisle – and Uncle Carlisle was just how Uncle Carlisle was. There'd be no tears from him. 'Lil' man, calm down. There's still work to be done,' he said. He was grinding me again but in a good way. He knew the hard work was to come. Then I rang my godfather, Denton Hoyte. My real father didn't care but I knew Denton did. I called him Pops: he was like a father figure for me. I was lucky to have these two around to inspire me.

Jeremy Alleyn was quick to get in touch when he heard the news. He was one of the guys from Empire Cricket Club. After meeting me when I was six years old, Jeremy had given me my first cricket ball. He laughed as we talked about how I told him I'd open the batting for the West Indies. My call-up meant a lot. He told me I'd made his day, month and year.

But there were still formalities that needed to be done. I was soon to be a full West Indies international – but I was still on the army programme. I had to report to camp, just as all the other guys did, in the morning. Except this time there was no toilet-cleaning, 4am runs or inch-perfect bed folding. I wanted to see Springer, Dowridge and everyone else there to relay the news. I was set for the big stage.

Many people said a lot to me after I was called up: brilliant words, moving words, inspirational words. The head of the BDF football programme, an Irishman by the name of Mr Kevin Millard, gave me an envelope with $1000 in to take my girlfriend at the time out for a meal. 'Anyone who works as hard as you deserves it,' he said. I insisted he shouldn't. I tried to give it back but he was having none of it. Man, this was his own money: I couldn't take it but he wouldn't take no for an answer.

But Dowridge's talk that day hit home the most. He said he knew I was West Indies material when he first met me in 1997 – and now I was there. Even when I was rejected, and rejected, and rejected, Dowridge stood by me. Spurring me on, the great Commander Dowridge. The man who supported me so much when my friend Crashy so tragically passed, the great Commander Dowridge. Crashy's face was missing that day at the army camp, but his spirit wasn't. I knew he'd be the first to give me a hug. If only he was here to see it.

The West Indies team manager, Ricky Skerritt, welcomed me to the camp the next day and gave me my kitbag. I laid out the gear and pulled on my West Indies whites. I looked in the mirror. Man, I was proud. I slept in them that night. They were my pyjamas and, you know what? They were the best pyjamas a man could have. Here I was, wearing the West Indies badge to bed. It was a boyhood dream coming true – the most amazing of dreams.

But you see, I'd worn the badge before and it hadn't ended well.

I was thirteen when I stayed one time for the weekend at my

Uncle Carlisle's house. He had a cricket room at his place, full of all his gear. For me, it was heaven. A whole room for cricket: it was like a dream.

Uncle Carlisle had gone out and I did what I knew I shouldn't do. I went in there. And, worse still, I went rummaging into his kitbag. I wanted to find the shirt he wore for the West Indies but, instead, I pulled out a West Indies Test sweater. A real thick one; one you'd need on a freezing cold day at Old Trafford.

I couldn't resist the urge. I put it over my head and pulled it on. It felt so, so good. I was due to play for Garrison School later that day and I knew I just had to wear it. So I did. Man, I felt proud as I walked out on to that field wearing the West Indies jumper. It was an absolutely boiling day in Barbados, steaming hot, but here I was, young Tino Best wearing his Uncle's Test sweater.

We were up against the Grantley Adams Memorial School, who had some real quick bowlers. Worse still, we were playing on a really bad pitch. I felt like I was playing my very own Test match, making forty four not out, batting at six. It was a real dig-in day with twenty nine of my runs coming in singles. Proud as punch, I went home to my uncle's place happy.

Uncle Carlisle was in when I got back. I was desperate to tell him how I'd done but first I had to return the sweater. He had no idea I'd taken it, you see, and he couldn't find out. Uncle Carlisle shouted to me as I got in, 'All right, lil' man?' That was what he called me. I was his little man. And he'd always give me a warm greeting.

I rushed into the cricket room. Before I'd even had chance to open the bag, Uncle Carlisle was standing there behind me. I'd been caught red-handed.

He was livid, I could tell – absolutely fuming.

'Tino, why did you take the sweater? Why?'

'Because I wanted to be like you,' I said. But he was mad.

I was thirteen, young and embarrassed. I wanted the ground to swallow me up. My uncle was getting right into me. I apologised and said it wouldn't happen again but he was disgusted. For the rest of the night I said nothing. I ate dinner, showered and watched TV without a word. I'd let my hero down. I felt like I'd betrayed him.

Later that night he shouted for me to come downstairs. Another chance for him to grind me.

I went into my uncle's bedroom to find him – except there was no grinding. Instead, he stretched out his hand and said, 'This is for you.' In his palm lay the old-time West Indian badge. The land, the stars, the coconut tree: there it was. Stunned, I took it from him. It was one of the sweetest things I'd ever been given.

'This is yours, Tino. This is a symbol of excellence,' he said. 'This is your inspiration. I want you to have your own badge. This is your freebie. Now work for the next one.'

To this day, I still have it. I keep that precious badge in my Bible. I will never, ever lose it. I could have been given a scolding. He'd made me feel so bad – then he made me feel so good. West Indies cricket is all about hard work and a legacy. I'd been given this badge in 1995 for free. In 2003 I'd been handed one that was all my own.

I laughed to myself that morning. Here I was, all alone in a hotel room, cleaning my teeth in my whites!

I'd have to wait for my big chance. In the second Test I was water boy and it didn't go well. Ricky Ponting hit 206, Darren Lehmann made 160 and Adam Gilchrist scored 101. Welcome to Test cricket. Four of our boys made centuries: Merv Dillon, Pedro Collins, Vasbert Drakes and Marlon Samuels. Centuries of the wrong kind, that is. All of them went for more than 100 as the Aussies made 576-4. We dug in but lost by 118 runs to go 2–0 down in the series.

The third Test came and we were back home in Barbados. With the four-match series almost gone, there were calls for new blood. I'd knew I'd be in.

The day before, in the team meeting, it was confirmed. Omari Banks and I had made the side and we'd be making our debuts together. Omari was a useful all-rounder – the first player from the Leeward island of Anguilla to play Test cricket for the West Indies. It'd be me and him versus the Aussies.

I rang all the important people. Mum told me she'd be there – of course she would: she was my rock. The entire army programme were down there from 8am. I let Brett Lee know I was in too. We were staying at the same hotel and I rang his room on the internal phone line. I loved the man and he was so delighted for me. See you on the pitch, Binga. I knew that, in a few hours' time, he could be trying to knock the living daylights out of me.

Our opponents were one of the best sides ever to play the game. It wasn't going to be easy. We were encouraged to stick to our game plan that got us where we were but, even still, there were a few vital instructions.

For Steve Waugh, we wanted to get the ball inswinging from outside the off-stump. Hayden, we'd go at. But the one key for me was aggression. Brian told me never to sacrifice that. I was an out-and-out quick bowler and I should never drag that back to bowl a line and length. Vasbert Drakes was in the side to do that. It was my job – and the fit-again Jermaine Lawson's job – to put it up the Aussies.

Brian won the toss and decided to field. The Kensington Oval – my backyard – was jam-packed. The crowd was screaming for the local boy and I had ball in hand ready to bowl my first over in Test cricket.

Lawson's first had gone for six and Hayden was on strike for the second. Mum was probably screaming away for me but I had blocked out everything. I was out in the middle and no one could help me.

I gave it everything: stormed in; pounded in as Tino Best does. I held nothing back. There were no nerves, just the pressure to do well for myself. People said I was the next Malcolm Marshall before I'd even played a Test. I just wanted to be Tino Best.

My first over went for ten. I put down a couple of bouncers and Hayden pulled one just wide of Brian and he couldn't get to it. The next two overs went for nine and that was my first spell done: 3–0–19–0. Not the best of starts.

A few overs later and I was back on at the Joel Garner End – and I came so close to getting my first Test wicket. It would have been a stunner too: RT Ponting.

I charged in again, trying to break the speed-of-sound barrier. Ponting drove hard and nicked it to gully. Yes! My first Test wicket. Shiv Chanderpaul was there to gobble it up. It was too good to be true. My first wicket: the great Ricky Ponting. Shiv had a decent pair of hands but then disaster. He downed it. Shiv had grassed it. Man, I was so, so hurt.

I couldn't help but think of playing for Barbados. If Sulieman Benn was in gully, there'd be no way he'd drop it. The big 6 foot, 7 inch Suli, with his giant hands, doesn't drop them. I was there, in Barbados, just wishing for my Barbados team-mates. And there, in that moment, was one of the huge difficulties in playing cricket for the West Indies. You are all from different nations, with different cultures and from different backgrounds. If Suli had dropped it, I'd have had guys there putting an arm round my shoulder. We were all Bajans; all in it together. They'd tell me I got the batsman to make one mistake and I could get him to make another. We'd all be together as one.

Brian was supportive. Vasbert, the only other Bajan in the side, was too and Jermaine Lawson was always good to learn from in the nets. But the others, not really. It wasn't even lunch on day one of my Test career and I'd had my first insight into why playing for the West Indies is so hard. It didn't hurt me – the lack of support – but it was an eye opener. In many ways, my debut Test was the hardest cricket match of my life. Don't get me wrong: these aren't selfish people. They're just so focused on wanting to play their best that it's hard for them to see the bigger team picture.

That day, I didn't have Courtney or Floyd to support me. Behind the stumps was Carlton Baugh – and he was from Jamaica. It just wasn't the same. It was my first big international match and I felt lonely. I felt totally on my own out there. The Aussies were a good – no, great – side. That was one problem but the lack of support from my team-mates was a bigger one. I know we were 2–0 down in the series, which didn't help, but no one said anything.

It was tough on the field and tough off it. I'd replaced Merv Dillon in the side to make my debut and he was a real senior figure. People were even saying he was the man to fill Courtney Walsh's boots when he retired. Merv played 38 Tests and 108 ODIs for the West Indies but that match he never, ever had a conversation with me. Not once. I don't know if he was intimidated that I was coming for his place but that bothered me.

He'd been dropped for me and didn't encourage me one bit. I didn't need it, I wasn't begging for it, but it would have been nice for a senior West Indian bowler, who was still with us in the camp, to acknowledge I was there. He didn't even speak to me or offer me a drink of water. Something simple like that would have been nice.

I watched Merv play when I was younger and I used to think he was one of the best bowlers but he just saw me as a rookie and he gave me the rookie treatment. I got home and thought that night that, whatever happened, I would never, ever be like that.

Off the field it was tough too. I was down at third man in front of the Hall and Griffith Stand for a spell in that match. There was one lady, above all the others, heckling me.

'I came here to see you and you're a massive disappointment,' she shouted. OK, fair enough, but I'm young, making my debut and anyone who knew anything about cricket knew I could bowl. They'd have seen it at this very ground. If she'd have followed Barbados, she would have known. Then she carried on.

'You made me waste my money. You're no good.' What the heck?

She's just abusing me for no reason. Why would you disrespect me in my first game, seriously? A few minutes later I shut her up. Ponting hit one down to third man and I swooped round like a heat-seeking missile. I fielded the ball, launched it into Baugh and he didn't have to move. The bails were off and Ponting, attempting a second run, was gone. I'd got him – eventually.

I got no support when I had him dropped but, that moment, I was mobbed. The lads were elated, high fiving me and saying what a big arm I had. I'd done something to show I belonged. I'd done something to inspire. That day was a wide awakening to what Test cricket was really like – but that moment made me feel like I belonged.

It didn't get much better than that. Australia racked up 605 for 9 before they declared. I bowled twenty overs, no wicket for ninety nine, in that first innings. Man, it was hard. Omari, my fellow debutant, didn't do well either. He picked up 3 wickets but was hit for 204 runs in 40 overs. That was the most runs ever conceded by a Test debutant.

The pitch was just too slow. Afterwards Steve Waugh came out and said it was one of the most docile he'd ever played on – and he played some 168 Tests. Brett Lee, Glenn McGrath and Jason Gillespie were steaming in as the Aussies replied but even I had no problems playing them. I was a bowler, playing on my debut... imagine what it was like for the batsmen.

I did have a bit of fun, making twenty not out in the first innings and smashing Brett Lee back for four over his head. He told me to get ready for a broken fucking rib after that. I loved it, absolutely loved it. The man was my idol and he was striving so hard to knock me over. I hit a beautiful sweep shot off Stuart MacGill too, for four. It wasn't all bad.

We lost that one by nine wickets. I made a duck as we followed on and the Aussies needed ten minutes to knock off the eight runs for victory to clinch the series.

I rang Courtney Browne after that game. He'd played international cricket and he knew what it was all about. I was down so told him how hard I found it and how I didn't feel like I had a support structure. He just told me to keep my mouth shut, respect each and every one of my team-mates and hang tight in there. It would get better, he said.

The next Test match, in Antigua, I was dropped for Merv Dillon. He took two wickets in the first innings, four in the second innings and was smiling and happy again. I'll never be like that. I wasn't bitter or angry about it because, when you're a rookie, anything goes. I was being sacrificed for a senior player and I wasn't thinking it was unfair – it was right. But the fact that he had snubbed me so badly pissed me off.

That game we pulled off one of the greatest chases in West Indies history, making 418 to win the Test in the fourth innings. Sarwan and Chanderpaul both made hundreds and Omari Banks and my Barbados mate Vasbert Drakes finished it off. Wow. Chanderpaul had to have injections in his finger and he went through so much pain to score that hundred. I have so much respect for him for that.

That debut Test was an eye-opener for me. I had a lot of work to do on my action and only when I saw it consistently on TV could I see how flawed it was. The West Indies just wanted two 90 mph bowlers and no one checked my action or how it'd hold up. They just wanted pace. I wasn't up to standard. I lacked control and consistency and bowled too many loose balls.

But my first Test was still an amazing experience. The Aussies didn't give me much chirp but that's because I was a rookie. To be honest, I was so taken aback by their humility. Guys like Brett Lee and Andy Bichel spent time to sit down and talk to me about my action. There'd give me little pointers and answer my questions. Huge respect to them for that. They were awesome cricketers and awesome human beings.

After that series, I went back to the BDF Sports Programme, where I heard one or two guys say it'd be the only Test match I would ever play. These people didn't know me. They think because I don't do well on debut that I'm going to give up? Your insults inspire me. I was cool with that. I just laughed at them.

But weeks later, the haters were in their element. I sat in my bedroom, staring at the ceiling, feeling so helpless after I'd just been dropped from the squad to face Sri Lanka. It was heart-wrenching. I'd played one Test and I felt I needed another opportunity to at least be in the mix. I felt I was the number-one bowler in the Caribbean in 2003 and that I should have got more than one chance – but no.

I started blaming everyone. 'People don't like me,' I thought. 'People are out to get me.' That's what I was saying to myself. It was never my fault. I did an interview with Ezra Stuart, who works for the *Nation* newspaper in Barbados, and he was saying he felt I'd got too big for my boots; that I felt I was better than everyone. Hearing stuff like that hurt even more. These people didn't know I was working my butt off to get back in the team. There was no first-class cricket between May and December. I couldn't be taking wickets if I wasn't playing games. What was I supposed to do?

I called Browney, my go-to man. Courtney said I needed to sort my action out. It looked like I was directing *The Three Tenors* because my arms were everywhere. My head was all over the place too. I knew I needed to be seen to be doing something and I knew I had work to do.

Browney told me how it was, which is just what I needed. Fortunately, I had another awesome human being to help: Wayne Daniel. I met him at Sheraton Centre Shopping Mall in Christ

Church, Barbados, totally by chance. There I introduced myself and offered to pay him to help me with my action – but Wayne's a true gent and he wouldn't take a penny.

'I will work with you for free,' he said. 'You have talent. You don't need to pay me. Maybe Lee or Akthar can bowl faster than you but no one else.' With that, he said he'd be willing to work with me every day. I was so grateful.

Wayne was a breath of fresh air. I was swept off my feet by his humility. I'd grown up seeing him on TV and I knew he'd played at Middlesex for years with close to 1,000 first-class wickets to his name. He'd played in the World Series too – a true legend. He was a folk hero to young fast bowlers.

Wayne got me tighter and worked hard on my run-up and my load. He got my shoulders and arms better aligned and my weight going right behind the ball. For five or six weeks he was with me every day. He came to the army camp to train with me and got me firing again. It was amazing. He got me bowling the quickest I'd ever bowled – and more consistently. Before I may have been between 85 mph and 91 mph. After Wayne's work, I was between 89 mph and 96 mph.

I'd never been coached like this in my life. Yes, we had coaches for teams but Wayne was my own personal coach. He got me grooving my action, time after time. He'd want me to practise in the shower, getting my body used to the process. He'd have his baseball mitt with him, coaching by his home in St Philip, at Rices Cricket Field or at Melbourne Cricket Field, where I grew up.

Wayne was a Godsend. We went for a four-week training camp at the Paragon military base and he'd come up there, be in the nets with me and continue his hard work. It was all with coach Springer's blessing, of course. He was delighted that Wayne was there for his young fast bowler. Sir Garfield Sobers was welcomed into the Barbados ranks but I don't know if other legends were encouraged by the Barbados Cricket Association to do likewise. If they weren't, I don't know why. This man Wayne Daniel was making me awesome.

Now I had to prove I wasn't a one-Test wonder.

CHAPTER NINE

MAKING A FAST BUCK

MS Dhoni: the highest-earning cricketer on the planet. India captain, former Chennai Super Kings captain, national heart-throb. Sponsored by Reebok, Pepsi and Sony. American business magazine *Forbes* had him down as earning $26.5 million by the age of thirty four.

Second top earner is Sachin Tendulkar, the Little Master. Gautan Gambhir's in third, Virat Kohli fourth and Virender Sehwag fifth. Those five have earned over $70 million between them. Wow.

Me? I reckon I've earned £1.5 million playing cricket. I've been playing fifteen years, give or take, so it's roughly £100,000 a year, which is OK. Let's get this straight: I don't play cricket for the money. I play cricket for the love of the game; for the adrenaline rush of steaming in and bowling at 90 mph and for representing my country. The cash is good and it's a nice amount, of course. I'm grateful for every bit of it.

There's a lot of talk about what cricketers earn. The Indian Premier League is the biggest cricket tournament on the planet. Watched by millions around the world, funded by millionaires. Players get put in an auction and, if more than one franchise wants you, you're cashing in. MS Dhoni's salary for IPL 2015 was $3 million alone. Yuvraj Singh banked a $2.67 million deal – and David Miller earned $2 million. He's not even played a Test for South Africa. There are huge amounts on offer.

Many have earned more than me, many have earned less. If I'd have broken through ten years later I could have earned a fortune playing Twenty20 around the world. The money is going up, up and up. It's staggering now – but I'm not bitter at all. My generation earned far more than my uncle's generation, for example. No doubt in ten years' time it'll be up even more. It's one of those things. I'm just grateful for what I've had.

Every player ever born will wish they were born later. My uncle works in a bank now but, if he'd been playing in this modern day, he'd have made a fortune. He used to smash it. Just ask anyone in the Kensington Oval that day he made a hundred against England. I can just imagine it: Uncle Carlisle, playing in the IPL, commentating on his own innings! He'd be great with one of the microphones on.

Starting out, I was on $195 for a four-day game for Barbados when I was twenty. There was no contract and you'd only get paid if you made the final thirteen. It was good money at the time. I'd earn $900 a month with the BDF Sports Programme too, so I was never short. It meant I could help Melissa, give Tamani anything he needed and look after myself too. I wasn't bad off.

My main income was from the BDF Sports Programme, which was my first job. I didn't have one as a kid and only picked up money playing the odd tape-ball tournament. I wasn't alone in not relying on cricket. Everyone in the Barbados team had a regular job, providing they weren't playing for the West Indies. That's where you have to be if you want to earn any money at all while playing in the Caribbean. I realised that pretty early. I'd go to Courtney Browne's villa or Sherwin Campbell's house and see what they had – and I'd want the same.

I wasn't driven by cash but I wanted to earn a good living. There's no better feeling than playing for your country but the money is always nice too. I knew that, if I wanted a nice car or a big house, I'd have to play for the West Indies. I couldn't afford that playing just for Barbados.

Courtney played sixty six times for the West Indies between 1995 and 2005. Sherwin played 142 games. But even still, they had second jobs. Courtney worked at a telecommunications centre for Cable and Wireless, while Sherwin worked in the law office. Philo Wallace – forty games for the West Indies – worked in the government. OK, Sherwin only started working towards the back end of his career when he fell out the West Indies team but he still had to earn his corn.

That's despite these guys earning more than the rest of the team. Back in 2002 the West Indies players used to earn something like $395 a game for Barbados. The captain would earn $650. We'd get no bonuses either. It was a straight fee to play. Not that I needed a bonus to try harder or bowl quicker. That's never been my nature. Bonuses were nice when I got them in my career – of course they were – but they were far from the be-all and end-all. Cricket is about winning first – not money.

Saying that, I used to love it when the Barbados treasurer came down with the brown envelopes on a Friday evening. He'd bring them in to the manager and he'd come and put them in your locker. Those days I'd be smiling away, feeling like a millionaire!

The money has improved now. I think you get a retainer of something between $15,000 and $25,000 if you play for Barbados. The match fees, on top of that retainer, are $1,300 a game.

I'd pick up $195 a game back in the early days and I topped up my money with a sponsorship deal with Smasher. They gave me £1,000 a year to wear their pads, gloves and spikes. I'd use their bats too under the same contract.

Except the money was a bit of a sticking point for us bowlers. The batsmen used to get all the big deals and the bowlers would get far less. Batsmen were seen as far more glamorous. Fast bowling is the hardest job in the world and I think we should be paid on a par with the batters. The fact that Dale Steyn and Mitchell Johnson have managed to get $1-million deals in the IPL shows just how good they are. Both of them are top bowlers. Massive respect to them.

I went on to move from Smasher to Gunn & Moore. The managing director, Peter Wright, had given me a bat as a kid and had told me to be like my uncle. Later, he remembered me and sponsored me from 2006 for £3,000 a year. I'd use a Gunn & Moore Maestro but, even still, some batsmen elsewhere would earn like £80,000 or £90,000 a year. The bowlers were never the ones in favour.

A few years later, I came over to New Balance. I loved their cricket shoes and I thought they were the best in the business. But again, I didn't get any big sponsorship deal like the batters. Us bowlers just didn't really earn a slice of the money. Man, I wish I'd been a batter! The young Tino Best, who wanted to open the batting for the West Indies, was so right. He knew best!

I had deals with Puma, Nike and Asics too but they didn't earn me any money. They were just for free shoes. I had a deal with Spartan for bats too. Again, I didn't get paid for that.

The more I did in the game, the more I earned. In my first West Indies A team tour in 2003 I picked up $4,000 for two and a half months of work. I'm careful with my cash but, to be honest, I can't even remember what I did with that.

My first West Indies pay cheque, also in 2003, was for three Test matches. I earned around $3,800 a Test – despite only playing one – and that was topped up with sponsorship money from

Cable and Wireless. That's where the main cash was earned, through the sponsors.

For three Tests, I took home something like $60,000 – and $50,000 of that was through sponsors. Overall, it equates to $120,000. The first thing I did, on the advice of my mum, was to go and buy land for $100,000. The land was worth $120,000 dollars but Sir Garfield Sobers came in and helped negotiate them down to $100,000. He spoke to the people and sorted me out. What a good man. A cricketing genius – and a bloody good bloke.

To be honest, I wanted to go out and buy a Mercedes Benz or a BMW at that time. I was twenty one and I was driving around in a little Toyota. I wanted an S Class or a convertible but mum knew that land was the best way to make my money. So that was that: mum told me not to be flashy and my first pay cheque was gone.

There was one time where I did allow myself a bit of a treat though. In 2004 I got myself a $10,000 Breitling watch. It's one of the only times I've really treated myself. I love it and want to use it as a bit of a family heirloom. I want to give it to Tamani for his twenty first birthday and I want him to pass it down to his son or daughter. He could say, 'Pops worked hard and gave me this watch and now it's yours.' It would mean a lot to do that.

Brian Lara took most of the money that went to the West Indies players. The captain and the senior players used to be looked after the most. So him, Chanderpaul, Gayle and Sarwan: the big four. There was no resentment; it's just the way it worked. I certainly didn't begrudge them it and I don't think anyone else did either; I saw no hard feelings among the squad because they earned more than the rest.

The money went up when Digicel came in. I started to earn $18,000 a Test: $5,000 for playing and then another $13,000 in sponsorship. There's been a lot said about money in the West Indies and players getting paid, or not getting paid, on time. I can say now, I always got paid – and I never had a problem with them at all.

I never played at a World Cup so I couldn't tell you how much that's worth. But I have played in two ICC Champions Trophy competitions. I may have only played one game in each but they were decent earners: $50,000 or $60,000.

From the tour to England in 2012, when I smoked ninety five at Edgbaston and for which I stayed on for the one-dayers, I brought home maybe $100,000. The last tour I went on, to New Zealand, I earned $150,000. Compare that to back in my first days as an international cricketer and you can see how things have changed. The money has improved tremendously and I think it'll keep going that way. If it does, and my son Tamani makes it, I hope he gets a big contract. Then he can start looking after Dad! He's a batsman too... Let's hope it stays that way!

Once I got paid for tours, I always used to save the money. My uncle was an economist and having him in my corner helped. I was always in a good space with my Uncle Carlisle. On the other hand, my dad had nothing. I spent money on him from time to time, getting him stuff, but he just sold it for drugs. He's a sad fellow.

I was well out of favour with the West Indies in 2008 – and I simply needed money. I gave a pretty damning interview with the *Nation* newspaper in Barbados, where I said just that. I'd just signed up to play in the unsanctioned Indian Cricket League and questions were being asked.

I told a reporter, 'It's a little sad, but I can't go to the supermarket and say that my name is Tino Best, I bowl at ninety miles an hour, I want $400 in groceries. People will ask me if I'm going mad. It is about securing myself and my family. It was a very tough [decision], but at the end of the day you have to live. I'm not a carpenter, a lawyer or a doctor. I'm a cricketer. I have to apply my trade to survive.'

The West Indies coach at that time was a good man named John Dyson but he just didn't fancy me. Apart from playing for Barbados, league cricket in England and a bit with Lashings – a legends side in

England – I didn't have an income. I'm a tradesman and cricket is my living. I needed money to get food for Tamani.

In truth, the ICL deal was a no-brainer. I was out of the West Indies team and I wasn't earning any real money of note. My three-year deal with the Mumbai Champs was worth $250,000 a year, which was huge.

I played a season there and got paid around $200,000 for my six games with them. But then it all collapsed and I never saw any more of the money. It was a huge shame – and not just for my bank account. The food was great, the culture was too and we had 80,000 people turning up at every game. It would have been nice to have two more seasons of that.

I landed a deal with the Sylhet Royals to play in the Bangladesh Premier League in 2013. It was worth $75,000 but I got called up by the West Indies and never got a penny. I didn't bowl a ball for them. In the end, I'm glad. I wasn't too keen about it and my fears were justified.

I'd read a lot of stories about the players in the BPL not getting paid properly. In 2012, the Federation of International Cricketers' Association even advised players to skip future editions of the tournament. They released a statement saying that at least twelve overseas players were yet to receive their full payments, which amounted to over $600,000.

The FICA's chief executive, Tim May, said, 'The Franchises and the Bangladesh Cricket Board [BCB] have been in breach of contract for nearly two and a half months. We have given them every opportunity to settle these amounts and they have continually responded with a series of broken promises and empty public pronouncements.

'It goes without saying that FICA will be strongly recommending to all players, both in and outside Bangladesh, that they should not contemplate participating in this tournament in the coming years.'

Chris Gayle and Shahid Afridi were two of the stars that went out there but I'm glad I avoided all that. I was only really keen because it would have been a chance to play more cricket and earn more money. Who doesn't want to do that?

As for the IPL, I've come close to playing in the tournament a few times. I thought I would be signing for the Rajasthan Royals and Sunrisers Hyderabad, both in 2013. Tom Moody was coach of the Sunrisers and he told he wanted me there. In the end, it broke down. I've no idea why. I think the owners wanted another player or there was a problem with the budget, or something like that.

I tried again in 2014. I put my name in the hat for the auction but didn't pick up a bid. Not that I was alone. Ross Taylor, Tillakaratne Dilshan, Angelo Mathews and even my old mate Brett Lee didn't attract any either. Brett still had it too. A few months later, in his last game of professional cricket, he nearly pulled off the impossible in the Big Bash final. Perth Scorchers needed one off the last three balls against Sydney Sixers. Brett (or 'Binga') then took two wickets in two balls and just missed out on a hat-trick as they lost. It would have been the dream finish. Even though he wasn't good enough for the IPL, apparently.

Other top T20 players like Mahela Jayawardene, Cameron White, Brad Hogg and Azhar Mahmood didn't get any offers in the initial auction. I am a little disappointed I didn't get to play in the IPL. I don't know if it's because I played in the Indian Cricket League that they didn't really want me. On days I was in the auction I used to follow it on Twitter and see 'Tino Best goes unsold', which was a shame. I was still playing for the West Indies at the time so it wasn't the be-all and end-all. It wasn't like if I didn't go with the IPL I'd be starving. So I was disappointed, yes, but everything happens for a reason.

Closer to home, my first year's earnings in the Caribbean Premier League, in 2013, were brilliant. I was playing for the West Indies at the time and there was a rule that no West Indies player could go for less than $50,000 a season in the auction. Happy days. St Lucia Zouks paid $95,000 for me for seven games of the tournament but we didn't do too well. In fact, we finished bottom.

The next year I'd been dropped by the West Indies and I got a contract with the Zouks for $10,000. How does that work? One year worth $95,000, the next I was worth $85,000 less. It was worse for my mate Fidel. He was playing for Trinidad & Tobago Red Steel and earned just $5,000. The year before he had a deal for $70,000.

And if we thought that was bad, 2015 was a nightmare. I went into the auction and picked up no offers. Fidel got a contract worth $10,000 and Kemar Roach wasn't bought. How the heck? He was twenty six and one of the best bowlers in the West Indies. How had he not got a contract? Sometimes there's just no respect for senior West Indies players playing in the Caribbean.

I think half the reason I didn't get a deal in 2015 was because of my feud with Kieron Pollard. I'm not saying he had an influence but the incident, when we were involved in a mini-brawl in a lift, tarnished my name. Even still, I didn't do anything wrong but the damage had been done. The Caribbean Premier League is the biggest sporting tournament in the Caribbean and I was the most successful fast bowler in the region. Between 2002 and 2013, I don't think anyone would have taken more wickets than me. Not even Pedro Collins, who took a hatful. Yet I didn't get a deal.

In England I had a decent contract at Yorkshire in 2010. I played eight County Championship games – as well as the one-day and T20 stuff – and they took really good care of me. I think after tax I took home £40,000. That was brilliant for me. I wanted the opportunity because I wasn't playing Test cricket. Yorkshire is the biggest county in England and I just wanted to play at the top level. To be honest, they could have paid me $10 and I would have gone to Headingley.

We finished third in the County Championship. I took seventeen wickets at an average of forty two – not great. We missed out on reaching the quarter-finals of the T20 and, although we got to the semi-finals of the one-day tournament, I was gone by then.

I might not have ever got that £40,000 though. I wasn't getting many wickets and the coach, Martyn Moxon, felt I needed a break. He was a good man, Froggy. That's what we called him. I don't know why but I reckon it was something to do with his big calves. He left me out against Warwickshire but I wanted to play, as I felt I was just getting my rhythm.

We won the game and he came into the dressing room to high-five me as we celebrated. I wasn't in the mood though. I was proper pissed I wasn't playing. I didn't high-five him and he was livid. None of the guys could believe it. They couldn't believe I'd snubbed him.

Froggy called me into his office and went mad after that. He said he'd put me on the next flight if I ever disrespected him again. I laughed with Froggy and told him, 'Whenever you're ready, you can take me, Coach.' He just told me to get out after that. It was just a minor incident really. The county has a special place in my heart and so does Froggy. He's a top man despite our little disagreement that day. We didn't lose any sleep over it.

Living in Barbados is so much different to life in England. Our lifestyles are the complete opposites. In England they have mortgages. If you want a nice house, you'll go and get a mortgage – not in Barbados. I built my house with cash. It's worth $1 million now and I probably spent around $500,000 on it, building it up from scratch.

Playing international cricket for another country can be harder, I guess. In the Caribbean we live with our parents for longer so we can save money and build our own home. When we do, we have equity in our own house. If I lived in England and played for England, it'd be expected that I get a mortgage on a house with my first pay cheque. Then you're having to pay that off for years – even if you're not playing cricket. You're forever paying back to the bank.

Instead, in the Caribbean, if you could build a house for $1 million, it might be worth $3 million in ten years' time and you flip your

Above left: My young warrior Tamani Tino Best, with his mum Melissa.

Above right: Taken in 1998, after two months in the BDF Sports Programme. This is the first time I'd seen mum since I started.

Below: A very royal handshake: Meeting the Queen before our 2004 Test against England at Lord's was a huge honour.

WEDNESDAY, APRIL 16, 2003 BARBADOS, W.I. www.nationnews.com BDS$1

'ILL-FATED'

Union official: Government buildings, schools making people sick

GOVERNMENT BUILDINGS are seriously compromising the health of people who use them.

Orlando Scott, senior assistant general secretary of the Barbados Workers' Union (BWU), made this charge in the feature address of the 29th annual conference of the Barbados Union of Teachers (BUT) at Almond Bay Conference Centre on Monday night.

"The problem of workers falling ill when exposed to dust or other chemicals when repairs to schools or construction work are in progress, or workers becoming ill as a consequence of lack of or poor maintenance of buildings, pervades the entire Public Service," he said.

Speaking on the subject: **Striving For A Healthier And Safer Environment In Public Schools,** Scott said school personnel faced all the potential hazards found in normal indoor and office environments.

He cited issues of air pollution, heat, ergonomics problems from poorly-designed furniture, overcrowded classrooms and infectious diseases, among others.

"Teachers and students from the Louis Lynch Secondary School have been complaining for years about the effects of the emissions from an industrial plant . . . . Parkinson Secondary sits to the west of an industrial plant and one of the busiest highways in Barbados. I am told that some classrooms cannot be used because of the noise and constant emission of fumes from vehicles.

"Bay Primary has been identified by the BUT as a school where there are broken sheets of asbestos on the roof. The BUT points out that construction work has been ongoing at St Leonard's for five years and there have been several health and safety issues related to heavy construction on the compound."

He said Government had a responsibility to adopt in schools the same systems that were put in place in factories and offices to govern industrial relations, human resources management and matters like health and safety.

"The Ministry of Education must work far more closely with the ministries of Labour, Health and the Environment, relative to putting mechanisms in place to deal with occupational safety and health, environmental and public health issues that now confront schools in Barbados," he added.

TINO'S ON TOP OF THE WORLD.

Tino Best was overcome with emotion yesterday after receiving the news that he was called up by the West Indies selectors.

"I am totally elated. I am at a loss for words," the exciting Barbadian fast bowler said moments after hearing he was named as a replacement for Jermaine Lawson, who has been diagnosed with chicken pox, for the second Test against Australia starting Saturday.

"I have been thinking about a call-up, but I still cannot believe it. It has not sunk in yet. Right now I just feel like running the block."

Best's mother, Yvette, was just as delighted. She was jumping all over the place when she heard of her son's selection.

When **NATION** photographer Chris Brandis caught up with them at their Haynesville, St James home, Best greeted his mother with a big hug.

Please see also Pages 39A and 40A.

I made the front page of *The Nation* after my first ever Test call-up against Australia. One of the best days of my life – as you can probably tell from the way I'm hugging mum!

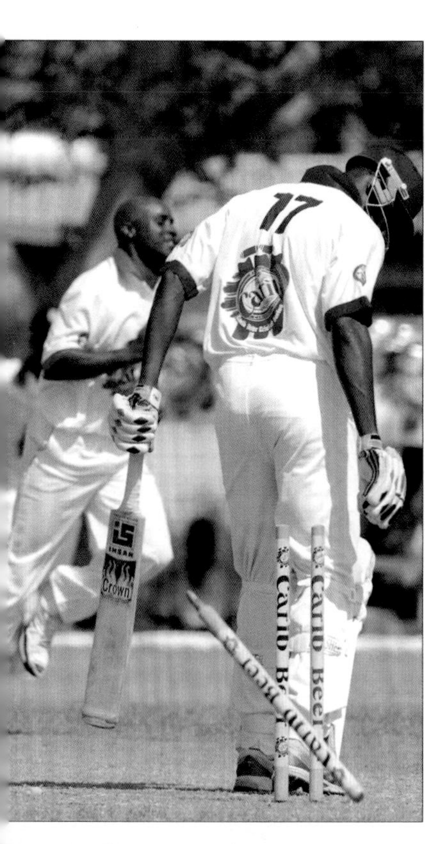

Above left: Just after I bowled Kieron Pollard. Believe me, that one felt good.

Above right: Here I am taking a tip from the Black Diamond himself, Wayne Daniel. I would not have liked to face him in his prime.

Below: Nothing gets the blood pumping like a well-aimed bouncer.

Above: Giving a pep talk to these amazing kids about drug abuse, cricket and choosing the right path in life. I've learned a little something about that last topic over the years.

© *The Nation*

Below: Me and my two special ones, Thalia and Tamani. They are everything to me.

money. If you have finished playing cricket and you are broke, you could sell the place and have $3 million to spend. You could bank $2.5 million then and build another smaller house with the rest of the money. Simple.

I was always smart with my finances. I have my mum to thank for that. She brought me up well, telling me not to get carried away. Her and Courtney Browne, my big brother with the West Indies, were so good to me. Thanks to them, I don't have any debts in my life.

I had a lot of old heads passing down knowledge to me. I knew that, if I played well enough for long enough, I'd be OK. The West Indies Players' Association (WIPA) used to have seminars where people came in and gave advice. It was nice support but not for me. My knowledge of being smart was taken from Courtney, Floyd, Mum and my Uncle Carlisle.

Thanks to them, I've never had a problem and I've never made many bad decisions. I lived with my mum when I broke into the West Indies team and saved up money to buy my own place. Then, when I could, I bought her house outright from the government so she owned it all. She had a few debts too, of around $20,000. I paid them off so no one would ever come looking for her. I didn't want people asking her for money, thinking she was the mum of a big international cricketer. During all this, she was still working in the hospital so she still had an income.

I didn't pay her rent so I felt getting the house was the right thing to do. As I earned more, I'd get one or two vacations for her. She is a modest woman, working herself, not needing my help, but I love to look after her. For her birthday I'd treat her to some nice white pearls or perfumes.

The fact that she has never asked for my support shows what kind of woman she is. She's amazing. She was always cool for herself, just like the rest of my family. They are all working people, doing jobs and having their own income. I'll look after Tamani the same. I tell him to go to school, do his work and get educated. A cricket career can leave you – you can get dropped – but education never does. That's what I preach.

You hear about people spot-fixing because of their families being in danger or something like that – earning a hell of a lot of money before they're caught. For a start, you never know what's happening in their personal lives, so it's hard to judge.

I'll tell you now: no one has ever, ever approached me to spot-fix. I think people saw me play so passionately on the field that they didn't bother. Everyone has a choice to make and people have done wrong. Cricket should be respected at all times and these people doing the spot-fixing must be very, very desperate. Never would I do that.

CHAPTER TEN

FROM THORPEY TO USHER

I knew there was only one way to get back in the West Indies national side after being dropped after one game – and that was to perform. All the netting in the world and all the practice bowling in the shower would mean nothing if I didn't bring home cricket's greatest currency: wickets. I had to do it: for my mum, for myself, for Wayne Daniel.

Our first game of the 2004 season against Guyana was a good one. I took one wicket in the first innings and I was on a hat-trick in the second, ending up with three. The wickets were nice but the game was good for other reasons too. I felt strong, the ball was coming out quicker and I could have bowled all day. We won too. A good start for the Best-Daniel double act.

The Windward Islands were our next opponents and I was full of positivity. Courtney Browne stood up in the team meeting and talked about how I was swinging the ball and how strong I looked with a still head in my action. Floyd Reifer, another of the senior boys with the best view in the house from first slip, echoed his words.

That game was a whirlwind. I was twenty two years old and I don't think I'd ever bowled as fast. I was as fast as a raccoon. I shot out the openers – Devon Smith and Romel Currency – before following that up with Rawl Lewis, a handy all-rounder, and my good mate Darren Sammy. Within the blink of an eye, I'd taken 4 for 33 and the Windward Islands were 113 all out.

If the first innings was good, the second was even better. We held a lead of 182 but it was all academic. Out went Devon Smith again – bounced out and caught at gully – and the rest folded like a pack of cards. I was rapid, express pace, but now it was so controlled. Bouncers were well-directed, inswingers were hitting their mark and outswingers were on song. Guys were ducking into pitched-up balls – that's how quick it was. Wayne Daniel watched the entire game and he, the perfectionist, even said I looked magnificent. It was the quickest he'd seen someone bowl since Patrick Patterson, he said. Patrick was the great fast bowler of the late 1980s who was far quicker than Malcolm Marshall.

Guys from the Barbados team that day still talk about that spell. Devon Smith's wicket was the start of carnage. I took seven for thirty three and they were all out for ninety two. Wow. It earned me my second man-of-the-match award for Barbados and I dedicated it to Wayne. Who else? I gave him my man-of-the-match trophy too.

My mum came down to watch that game. She made her way to the ground on the bus but, by the time she got there on day three, it was game over. At least she tried. She was so pissed I'd bowled the other side out. Even she, a non-cricketer, could sense I was firing. She knew me better than anyone and said I looked stronger and fitter than ever before.

That was the start of something special. Jamaica awaited me next and I felt invincible. It's my place, Jamaica, the home of the fast bowlers – and Sabina Park in Kingston was also home to the greatest match I've ever played in. I took five wickets in the first innings but still we were only seven runs ahead. Then, at 187 for 9 in the second, we were in real trouble.

But I came out and smashed it, putting on sixty four runs for the last wicket with Sulieman Benn. I wound up forty two not out, while Suli was caught for twenty two. Runs, batting at eleven… it wouldn't be the first time that happened for me. With us defending a score of 258, against our fierce rivals, everything was on the line.

Courtney had said I'd get back into the West Indies team if I performed there and then – and I did. In, in and in I charged, baying for blood. I was hitting guys in the head, getting others caught gloving and running riot. I've never seen batsmen back away like they did here. I was running everyone off the pitch. The Jamaican public couldn't believe it. They were in the ground that day, chanting my name, yet I was the enemy. Courtney Browne must have been thirty yards back behind the stumps and he was still taking the ball at head height. First slip was nearly on the boundary. There'd be no five-for this time but three for fifty three did the job.

Another win, another man-of-the-match award. The commentators were loving it. I remember hearing one say something along the lines of, 'Mark my words: Tino Best will be opening the bowling against England this summer. He's the quickest bowler we've seen for some time.' Wickets and runs, I'd won the game for the team. Browney said he'd never seen me this good. You know what? He was right.

That performance was the start of something special. It was the turning point. Seven games in the Carib Beer Cup, seven wins. The final against Chris Gayle's Jamaica, another win. I ended the season with 37 wickets, for 509 runs, at an average of 13.75, including three five-wicket hauls. Thanks, Wayne. I was a champion again.

I was expecting the call to get back in the West Indies team for the visit of the England team, as I'd knew I'd had a big year. So, when the call came, I wasn't entirely surprised. I don't know if the doubters from the army programme heard I was back but I do hope they did. Never write me off.

Since being dropped, the team had done well: a Test series win against Sri Lanka was followed by another in Zimbabwe. Although that was soured somewhat by a 3–0 thumping in South Africa soon after, where Fidel had no one bowling quick with him.

My old mate Makhaya Ntini, combined with Andre Nel and Shaun Pollock, took sixty seven wickets between them in that four-match series. Fidel, our leading wicket-taker, took eight. Ramnaresh Sarwan was our third-most successful bowler with six. Sarwan was a part-time leg-spinner, who was by no means the worst. He did have a handy knack of getting wickets and breaking partnerships, a bit like Carl Hooper, and he could come in and keep it tight. But the fact that he took that many wickets showed the other bowlers weren't supporting Fidel enough.

Brian knew Fidel needed support and, when he told me I was in because we needed another fast bowler, I was licking my chops. I'd worked hard and, coming off the back of the first-class season I'd had, I deserved it. But my success was really all down to Wayne. The call-up was as much about him as me.

The great man wouldn't accept any money, so I took him out for dinner with a girl I was dating, who was called Melissa Browne. She knew how much I appreciated everything he did and she suggested I bought him a really nice watch. So off I went to get him a beautiful Citizen, a really nice rose gold piece. I presented it to him and gave a speech to thank him so much for being there when the whole world had turned their back on me and when no one believed in me. I had the strong mother in my life but I had a whole lot of fathers – and Wayne was one of those.

The pre-series camp was in Jamaica, a place that held so many fond memories for me. Just arriving there and smelling the Jamaican air again was a relief. It was time for me to go again and I was ready to take on any challenge. The previous season I'd taken thirty nine first-class scalps but even I can admit some of them were lucky. I was so quick that I used to get guys out through shock factor. Some full tosses I ended up bowling took wickets. On my Test debut I'd been thrown into the deep-end and I wasn't good enough. Now my level of cricket was way up. I was a new, fine-tuned Tino Best.

And I was now part of a real group. I'd felt a bit of an outcast before but now it was like I fitted. I could turn to Corey Collymore, Pedro Collins or Fidel Edwards if I needed them. Ryan Hinds, another Barbados team-mate, was in that squad too. They were there to sound ideas off of. If I needed to know what they thought about a particular spell, or a delivery, I could turn to the other Bajan players and know they were there for me. On my debut, it couldn't have been further from that.

Brian told me I was due to face England, the old colonial master, in the first Test at Sabina Park the night before. I asked God for guidance, strength, to stay fit and avoid injury, and to bless my team-mates. I knew now I deserved to be on the biggest stage.

We started OK, winning the toss and making 311 with Devon Smith scoring 108 and my good friend Ryan Hinds hitting 84. I scored a handy twenty too, smashing a six off Ashley Giles before being given out LBW off of Steve Harmison. Never, ever was it out. Billy Bowden even apologised after the day's play when he'd seen a replay. Still, it was frustrating. It wouldn't have happened if I was a batter.

It was day two by the time I got ball in hand and the crowd were on their feet for me. 'Tino, Tino, Tino,' they chanted. I'd been away but now I was back – and I felt like the hometown hero. I started well, bowling rapid and I had Nasser Hussain and Mark Butcher fearing for their lives. At the same time, I wasn't giving much away.

I bowled four overs for five in my first spell, with a maiden in there too. The Ferrari now had a steering wheel. At the other end,

Fidel was getting them ducking and diving too. As we came in for lunch, the dressing-room attendant for the English came over to us and said how the whole team were nervy. They couldn't believe two guys as small as me and Fidel could be bowling at 94–95 mph. They thought it was crazy.

I knew then that I'd got them. Rain washed out the rest of the day but they would have a rough night's sleep thinking over what was to come. Fidel had cleaned up the top three of Trescothick, Vaughan and Butcher – not a bad trio to get rid of – but early on day three he pulled up with a side strain midway through his twentieth over. It was my time to lead the hopes of my country.

Nasser and Thorpey stood at the crease. The first day I'd said nothing. Unlike me, I know, but this was all to change. I knew we needed inspiration so I picked my fight.

'Hey, Thorpey, is this the great Graham Thorpe who has faced the best bowling all over the world? You're way past your best.'

He didn't like it. The great man took the bait from the rookie. In his deep, well-spoken voice, he retorted words to the effect of, 'Besty, I've faced better bowlers than you. I've faced all the legends.'

Brilliant: I'd got under his skin. So I bounced him, he missed and I eyeballed him. The crowd roared – they were right behind me. I hadn't a Test wicket to my name but I was up for the battle.

I told Thorpe I'd go round the wicket, break his rib and put him in a wheelchair. The adrenaline was going and I was baying for blood. I charged in again, round the wicket this time, as promised, and he went to pull again and missed. I laughed then went at him again: 'You're not great anymore, I'm going to hurt you.'

I ran in and went short once more – of course I did. What else is a quickie to do? Thorpe ducked his head, turned away as he pulled and a top edge flew up in the air. As that ball soared into the sky, everything froze. There may have been thousands of screaming Jamaicans but I could hear my own heart beating. It was an easy catch, in truth, and Adam Sanford comfortably took it. After thirty overs of Test match toil, I had my first wicket. I can still hear the TV commentary now.

'It's up in the air, it's down by fine-leg and it's taken,' Michael Holding, the West Indian great reported excitedly. 'Tino Best gets his first Test wicket. He has waited a very long time. You can see how elated he is.'

I couldn't contain myself. I felt so excited that my knees collapsed on to the Sabina Park turf. Chanderpaul was the first person on top of me and then Chris Gayle, Ridley Jacobs and Corey Collymore all followed. It was like we were celebrating a football goal. Jamaica was absolutely buzzing – and so was I.

Even Ian Botham, alongside Holding in the commentary box, enjoyed it: 'Well, there's lots of aggression, the bouncer in, this time not hooked with any control and it flies down to the fine-leg region. Sanford hardly has to move.'

Freddie Flintoff was in next but I had my eye on Nasser. The ball may have been sixty three overs old, and soft, but I only knew one way. I knew he didn't like the pace and no one wants it round their earholes. Just like his mate Thorpey, that's where he got it. With Sabina Park rocking, in I charged again, pride and passion pumping through my veins. This was my stage; this was my time.

I gave Nasser another short ball. He fended it and the leading edge popped up to cover where our sub-fielder David Bernard was waiting. I roared. Yes, another one baby: two wickets by lunch. That lunchbreak was one of the sweetest of my career. I'd taken my first Test scalps and they'd come against England – the team my uncle had made 164 against, 14 years before. These two guys I'd got were legends of the game; guys I'd watched as a child. It was a fairytale come true. From 193-3 to 209-5, we now had England in trouble. Now I wanted five.

Flintoff and Chris Read consolidated before we took the new

ball. With Fidel off the field and the wind in my sails, it was mine to do damage with. Read had been around too long for my liking. I told him I'd knock his head off before firing in a bouncer that had him in all sorts of trouble. He didn't pull or duck and he could only manage to loop it up to my Bajan team-mate Ryan Hinds for my third of the day.

Ashley Giles, Matthew Hoggard, Simon Jones and Steve Harmison were left. The crowd's on my side, it's a fast bowler's paradise and these guys are there for the taking. 'Tino, you have to get a five-for,' I thought. The first ball Hoggard faced, he backed away to square leg and defended a yorker. I wasn't impressed. I suggested he might not want to block them and that it'd be a better idea just to let it hit his stumps.

My words didn't really do the business. Not this time, at least. Hoggard ended up sticking around seventy one balls for his nine not out as Sanford, Hinds and a run-out cleared up the tail. Still, England's lead was only twenty eight and we were right in the game. Our bowling effort had been brilliant, especially with our leading man Fidel off the field. And, from a personal point of view, I felt at home. I was sure I was good enough for Test cricket and that day I proved it to everyone.

But from that point on, I don't know what happened. After three days of competitive cricket, we totally switched off. What happened next really hurt me. It blew away something so sweet and left me feeling so bad, as Steve Harmison absolutely ran riot. Between 2004 and 2006 he was the number-one bowler in the world and here he showed just why. I rated him highly as he generated so much bounce and shaped the ball too. This was the reason why he'd take over 200 wickets in Test cricket.

He blew us away in two hours, with only Devon Smith and Ridley Jacobs making double figures. I was one of his victims, for a duck, in his return of 7 for 12 off 12.3 overs. If ever you needed to be taught that Test cricket is tough and you can't switch off, here was our lesson. Five of us fell without scoring and, when Sarwan, Chanderpaul and Lara are three of them, you're in trouble. England knocked off the runs in ten minutes. Game over.

In the second Test, I continued where I left off, getting Trescothick (in both innings), Hussain (again) and Butcher. Still, it didn't do us much good as we lost that one and the next to go 3–0 down with one to play. With the series dead and buried, we went to the Antigua Recreation Ground in St John's with only pride to play for.

It was 10 April 2004, when Brian walked out with opposition skipper Michael Vaughan and won the toss and elected to bat. Freddie took out Daren Ganga early on and out went Brian at 33-1. Our side had been underperforming, struggling for runs with the bat and failing to make – and take – our chances with the ball. It made what followed the greatest innings ever played in cricket.

For 778 minutes Brian occupied the crease, facing 582 balls for a world-record score of 400 not out. There were extravagant cuts, lavish cover drives and beautiful hooks and pulls. This was a master at work. Hoggard, Harmison, Flintoff and Jones came at him with pace. Gareth Batty sent down fifty two overs of off-spin. But there was no removing the legend.

What was incredible about that innings, which spanned two and a half days, was that he was never tired. He had made 375 at the same ground against England in 1994 – a world record itself at the time – and he'd talk about how exhausted it had left him. Here he was just so relaxed and he made 400 of the easiest runs I've seen in my life. I've never witnessed a batsman masterfully get on top of bowling so smartly as Brian did here.

It was a joy to watch – and I was very nearly a part of it myself. Brian was 229 not out when Ridley Jacobs walked in at number 7. I was next in, knowing I'd need to stay around to help Brian reach the record if Ridley got out. And it looked like he had, when Michael

Vaughan bowled him, only for the umpire to signal for a no-ball. Ridley went on to make 107 not out, leaving me with pad rash watching history being made.

When people ask me who was better, Lara or Tendulkar, I find it impossible to really answer. Both guys are legends, geniuses, magicians with the bat, but what I do know was that innings was the best anyone has ever played. In terms of top sporting moments, only Usain Bolt winning the 100m and 200m at the London 2012 Olympics tops it for me.

I used to hear stories about Brian being this or that and people have tried to tarnish his reputation. Brian, the batsman, can never be faulted and he was a decent captain to go alongside it. Was he right to bat on and not declare when he scored 400? Yes, of course he was. A few days before, we'd just been bowled out for forty seven. Why wouldn't we try and put a big score on the board, ramp up the pressure and try and bowl them out twice? It wasn't like he was scoring at a slow rate either. Brian always put the team before himself. You can't ask for more than that from your leader.

His captaincy record is tarnished because he didn't have the greatest of results but I feel he did the best job he could with the players at his disposal. He was always encouraging me and the other young players and was always a splendid human being and a good gentleman. He took us out for dinners and worked his butt off to make us gel as a group. Having a load of different players from different countries together is always going to be hard and he recognised that and did all he could to make it work. In return, I always respected him, as he was such a genius. He will always be one of my favourite cricketers.

Like Brian, our coach, Gus Logie, worked hard to make us close as a group. He worked his butt off but I felt the batting line-up just didn't click for him. Chanderpaul struggled with depression that series and ended up averaging sixteen. He – and the rest of the batsmen – just didn't perform. I liked Gus a lot. He played over 200 times for the West Indies before being made coach and he did a terrific job. He was to guide the team to the Champions Trophy later that year and, although I didn't play a part because I was injured, I knew he was a real asset for us. He left by 'mutual consent' after that but I feel he was just discarded. And, to be honest, to get rid of someone after the success he had was just embarrassing.

I felt I had Nasser and Trescothick's card in the Test series and Gus must have liked what he'd seen. A return of twelve wickets at an average of twenty five was a good one. My economy – something I'd struggled with in the past – was good too: 3.13 an over. Suitably impressed, Gus handed me my first ODI cap a few weeks later when Bangladesh arrived in the Caribbean. I love playing all forms of cricket – I always have and always will – but I guess it was a little bit of a surprise in some regards. I'd not played a one-day match for Barbados, as they felt I was a four-day bowler. There was just no way past Pedro Collins, Corey Collymore, Ian Bradshaw and Sulieman Benn to get into the team.

Despite my lack of experience, the one-day series was a good one. We won 3–0, I took 6 wickets at an average of 9.5, including 4 for 35 on my debut, yet still it was strange. While my Test debut against Australia was a real fight and the England series was tough too, the Bangladeshis were just nowhere near that level. They were just running from the ball and didn't fancy the pace one bit. I don't think they expected to face people as quick as me and Fidel.

The Test series was a similar experience. I only got three wickets in the two games but I felt like I was all over them. The first was drawn in St Lucia on a real flat wicket. Even still, I felt far stronger and better equipped to bowl on that surface than the one I experienced on debut. That was all down to Wayne, of course. In the second, Sarwan went big with 261 not out to send us on our way to an innings and 99 runs win. Pedro Collins, with six wickets in the second innnings, did the damage.

My first experience of ODI cricket outside the West Indies came in England in 2004. New Zealand joined us for the three-way Natwest Series, which turned out to be one of the most amazing experiences of my life. Ian Bradshaw and Courtney Browne joined us in the squad for that, further boosting the Bajan contingent. Being in the squad just felt like I was at home again and those lonely first Test memories were long gone.

I didn't play every game and was saved for whenever they needed to let rip. I was given the opportunity to do just that against New Zealand at Cardiff's Sophia Gardens, a place that must have one of the flattest decks in the UK. I ended up going for forty eight in eight overs, without taking a wicket, but, if ever stats were misleading, here they were.

I sent the speed gun going berserk as I whizzed it down at up to 97 mph. The whole New Zealand team came out on the balcony to watch this short bloke, who they didn't know much about, send down some absolute bullets. Guys were just edging the ball off me and I got no luck whatsoever. I went at Craig McMillan and their great captain Stephen Fleming. I got Fleming to nick one but Carlton Baugh dropped it behind the stumps. David 'Bumble' Lloyd, up in the commentary box, was loving it. He was saying how quick this kid was and how he'd seen me in the Caribbean bowling serious gas.

The Sophia Gardens experience was great but playing at Lord's, facing England, was something else. Steeped in history, this was the place I'd dreamed about playing. Many of our side hadn't played there before and Brian did his best to keep us grounded. But how could he? Dwayne Smith and I stared in awe at the honours board. OK, you don't get on there for one-dayers but, damn, I wished my name was up there. Among the batsmen, the names of Viv Richards, David Holford and Gordon Greenidge sat proudly representing the West Indies. Courtney Walsh, Michael Holding and Malcolm Marshall, the man I was tipped to become, were among the legendary bowlers. My old mate Makhaya Ntini was on there too – twice.

The place was amazing and it's simply cricketing royalty. As a kid growing up in the Caribbean, despite being thousands of miles away, Lord's is where you want to play. The history, the fact the crowd is quiet as you bowl, the fact you could get to meet the Queen before a Test match. It's the biggest stage of them all. What a thing to tell your mates. 'I met the Queen!' It doesn't get better than that.

Living my dream at the home of cricket and fuelled by inspiration, I struck in my second over. I had the beating of Marcus Trescothick in the Test series shortly before and I knew I could get him again. And I did. I nipped a full, quick one back through his defence and England's danger man was gone, beaten by sheer pace. I was in heaven, a wicket at the home of cricket. I yelled at him, 'I'm the Best, mate. That's why my name's Tino Best,' and I pointed at the back of my shirt. Adrenaline pumping, chest-pointing, shirt-pointing.

Quarter of an hour later, Trescothick was reunited with his opening partner Michael Vaughan. I sent down a wider one which he flashed at and nicked off, caught by Ridley Jacobs. The captain gone – and I loved it. I yelled more of the same at him: 'Go inside, Vaughany. You're pretty average, mate.' The West Indies posse sitting in the Nursery End stand were ecstatic. The English were 27-2 and a packed Lord's was stunned.

Dwayne Smith got Rob Key soon after but from thereon it was all England – and all Flintoff and Andrew Strauss. They put on 227 in 31 overs – a record one-day stand for England – to set a target of 285. They murdered us and it was two of the best one-day innings I've ever seen. But I had a feeling in my stomach; I had a feeling we were going to get them. With Chris Gayle on our side, anything was possible.

I loved watching Chris. I played twenty five Tests and twenty six

ODIs all in all, so I knew him well. I'd been around, carrying water as the twelfth man, for another fifty, so I'd seen a lot of his game. I used to get so nervous watching him early, as he was vulnerable. But, if you didn't get him in the first overs, it could be a helter-skelter of carnage. He proved me right more often than not.

How do you get him out? Just be patient with the new ball. You have to nick him off by bowling good balls, just like you do to any other left-hander. If you miss your chance, he'll cream you. Bhuvneshwar Kumar is the only bowler I've seen that has had Chris's number. He swings the ball and is a real handful. But if the game isn't in India, I've always felt Chris could get big runs.

What came was perfection. Chris put on a masterclass, absolutely smoking the bowling to all parts. It was magnificent to watch: 132 not out. I've seen him play some incredible innings and this was, without doubt, one of the best of them. At the other end, Sarwan was at his busy best, milking Gough, Harmison, Anderson and Giles for eighty nine off seventy eight balls. Ricardo Powell, with thirty three off twenty two balls, finished the chase.

Until my dying day, I'll never, ever forget that game. We ran on to the Lord's field and mobbed Gayley. Nowadays, a chase of 285 isn't too daunting. Back in 2004 it was a huge ask. My hero Darren Gough, ever the gentleman, shook our hands and said, 'Well played, West Indies.' It meant a lot.

The celebrations went on and on. Brian took us out that night to the Movida Nightclub, just off of Oxford Street. Another example of what he used to do for us a group. Anyone who said he didn't care about the team is so wrong. All the younger guys – me, Smith, Bravo, Powell and Bradshaw – were on cloud nine. There was no Chanderpaul though. A great batsman, yes, but he doesn't go out.

That night, Brian came to the booth I was drinking in and told me to follow him. 'I've got someone for you to meet,' he said, so off we went. We walked across the dancefloor to a private area. Who was there? None other than international singing superstar Usher Raymond. What the frig? This was madness. 'Brian, you're a legend,' I thought.

Usher was doing his Confessions tour that year but he'd spent that day watching me. 'What's up, playboy?' he said with a beaming smile. His reception was so warm. I told him I was the best-looking man in the western hemisphere and it broke the ice and everyone laughed. He said he liked me, found me funny and we partied hard with some amazing girls around us. And I topped it off in the best way possible: with a lovely *ménage à trois* with two lovely ladies. Beating England at Lord's, partying with Usher and a threesome... it doesn't get much better.

Four days later, we were back at Lord's for the final to play New Zealand. They were a good one-day side, led excellently by Fleming. I went wicketless in the first game against them but I had hope. I felt I was on top of them and that my pace caused real problems. We were looking at footage in the team meeting when I stood up and stunned the room. 'I will get Stephen Fleming out tomorrow,' I said. And I meant it. I knew I could do it. I was beating him for pace at Sophia Gardens and felt that, on a better surface, I could get him out. 'Trust me,' I added. 'He's mine.'

Some of the guys laughed. Omari Banks told me to take it easy but I just knew I could knock him over. We won the toss and bowled and the first over with the new ball went well, just two off it. In the second over I had my breakthrough. Fleming, on seven at the time, nicked one straight to Chris Gayle at first slip. Joy! The big man's big hands would give me the Black Caps captain. Except, no: just when I needed someone to help me, he shelled it. I backed up what I said but I'd been let down by the fielders. At least I'd showed him I could cause a few problems.

The fielding let us down tremendously. I got Nathan Astle to cut one to Ricardo Powell at point, only for him to drop it. The cameras showed he'd downed the chance and Brian Lara had to call him back after it initially looked like he was out. I could have had so many more wickets in international cricket if we'd taken our chances. I feel we practised our fielding enough and, after all, no one goes to drop catches. We don't kill people when they drop one, as it's just one of those things. But telling everyone I'd get him, forcing the error and for the chance to go begging hurt so much. I knew I'd beaten him for pace.

I took 2 for 57 from my 7.2 overs and, admittedly, I went for a few. They used the speed of my bowling well but we still managed to restrict them to 266, which was gettable. Still, they started well, getting Gayley out early and the rest of the batsmen all followed as we slumped to a 107-run defeat. I'd miss the Champions Trophy, which we won, through injury and this proved to be my last ODI game for more than a year. If only Gayley had held that chance, it could have been so different.

But England wouldn't get off so lightly. I kept my place for the Test series and came into it in good form, having taken four wickets against Sri Lanka A in a warm-up game. Trescothick must have been sick of the sight of me when I steamed in at Lord's. He was an absolute legend, Trescothick, and his record speaks for itself. He scored more than 10,000 runs in international cricket and in some style too. He didn't move his feet that much but, if you criticise his technique, you've got to criticise everyone who has ever played the game. He was a brilliant cricketer but, within three overs, I'd got him again, firing in a short ball that beat him for pace and he could only spoon a catch up to Sarwan at square leg. I'd got Trescothick's number.

I could and should have had a second when Robert Key nicked me off to Devon Smith at second slip. He had his fingers under the ball when he took the catch, I'm sure of it. Replays backed that up but Devon put his hand up and said he didn't know if it was out and

Key was given a reprieve. He went on to score 221, in just short of five hours, hitting thirty one fours.

How Key scored a frigging double hundred that Test I won't know. I haven't been so pissed in my life. When you take a catch, you throw it in the air and celebrate. Devon should have done that. Key wasn't the worst batsman in the world by any stretch but there was no way he was good enough to score a double ton, even if the pitch was docile. It was just his day, I guess.

England made 568 before we hit back with 416, Chanderpaul scoring an unbeaten century while I was out first ball to Flintoff. Shiv was batting five and he drew criticism at times for that, with some saying he should bat higher up. I never really took much notice of that though. If he's happy there, so be it. Shiv is Shiv and he can make his own decisions.

I was eyeing up Trescothick again in the reply when injury struck. He hit my first two balls for four and all I could feel was a huge pain down my leg. I turned to the skipper and said, 'Brian, mate, my back is frigging done and my hamstring is on fire.' The scan the next day revealed I had a stress fracture of the back and I knew it was all over. All that was left for me to do was tough it out and walk out to bat in the fourth innings. One innings, then off home on the next plane to the Caribbean. Simple, no? Freddie had other ideas.

CHAPTER ELEVEN

BREAKING WINDOWS AND BREAKING RECORDS

I loved playing against England and I loved playing against Freddie Flintoff. He was one of the greats. What a man, what a player, what a competitor. I wish I could play against him every day for a hundred years. He's going to say something to you and come at you. Test cricket is made for guys like Fred. I was from a little village called Richmond Gap in Barbados. He was from the big city of Manchester. Playing for the West Indies gave me a chance to come up against him and I loved it. You get to represent your country and show what you can do. I love guys that take people on, like Fred.

Except that, when you're trying to tough it out with a big lad like Fred, it's not easy, especially when your body is in bits.

I had many fond memories of the place before I played international cricket. I knew all about Gordon Greenidge scoring 214 at Lord's in a Test match in 1984. GG was a Barbadian, like me, and he was lighting up the home of cricket. Wow. In 2002, while I was playing club cricket for a team in north Shropshire called

Madeley, I played at Lord's in a national knockout tournament. I was only with Madeley for five games before I got called up for the West Indies A tour. But I remember being so excited at being there. I was like a kid in a candy shop. We went to watch the second day of a Test against Sri Lanka. Andrew Caddick and Darren Gough were bowling at Marvin Atapattu and I was awestruck. Caddick just got so much bounce, so much carry, it was crazy. I just remember thinking it was so cool.

That day, Ian Botham was selling his book and I got one. I still have it now. One guy from Madeley told Beefy I'd play for the West Indies soon. He said, 'OK, yeah, good luck,' and barely looked at me. I laughed when I saw Beefy after that. Two years later he was commentating on me! 'I've met you before. You wished me good luck but you didn't really even see me,' I joked. He took it well.

It was on 26 July 2004 when Fred told me, through fits of giggles while I was batting, to mind the windows. For those who haven't seen it – and most have – Fred was basically trying to wind me up to play a big shot. He was in hysterics as he did it. It was my eighth Test match – my first at Lord's – and I was young and fiery. We were 203 for 7, trying to bat out a session and a half but I was in agony. I had a level-one or two stress fracture in my back and it was really hurting. It came about because I'd just been bowling so much. My body was letting me bowl fast but, despite all the work I'd been doing, I knew it wasn't that strong. In fact, the injury kept me out for nearly a year after that.

I was facing Ashley Giles, who was never a really big spinner of the ball. In the Caribbean I batted against him really well and I knew what he was all about. I wasn't a big fan of his. He didn't spin the ball much and in one game he got Brian Lara out twice. That annoyed me. How did he get the great man out? Brian was a legend and he wasn't good enough to do that.

I was pissed too. The English seemed to be getting the rub of the green on a few umpiring decisions, which annoyed me. I went out there thinking, 'I'll smash him into next week.' I'd hit him for six sixes, I thought. Come on, I was playing Test cricket at the age of twenty two and was living a dream. I felt like I had already conquered the world. Saving the game was the batsmen's job anyway. It shouldn't be down to me.

Fred was fielding at slip and I heard him say, 'Mind the windows.' I heard him that time but I wasn't paying it that much attention. A couple of balls passed by and he said it again. The thing was, I wasn't that bothered by what Fred was saying because of my back. We may have been trying to save the game – I was trying to save my body.

I had my bat in hand and in my head I was visualising what I wanted to do. I told myself I was going to play out a couple of balls and, on the sixth ball, I'd go up the wicket and chip Giles over the top. So I did: I missed it and got stumped. At least I didn't have to bat anymore – my back was killing me. I shouldn't have been batting at nine anyway. I had no chance of staying out there, I was in that much pain. I'd had painkillers but it made no difference – it was agony right down my back and my leg.

So I walked back into the pavilion and someone said, 'Did you hear what Freddie was telling you from first slip?' I was confused. I had no idea. 'What was he saying?' I asked. Then they told me he had been chirping me and the next ball I tried to slog and got out. He was going to get all the credit for talking me out, they said. I thought nothing of it.

We lost the Test and that was that. I went home the next week with the injury, it was that bad. It was then when someone said, 'Tino, Fred's sledge on you was one of the best sledges ever.' 'This again,' I thought. What were they talking about? What sledge? 'Mind the windows,' they told me. I was baffled. I heard him say that a couple of times but it was a few overs before I got stumped. So I went on YouTube and checked it out. And, yes, it does look bad.

Now what really happened is this: Fred told me to mind the windows four balls before I got out – NOT right before. It's been edited and put together to look like it is. I see it on TV shows now and have a laugh about it. Everyone has fun with it and I don't mind at all.

Fred is a legend and banter's banter. I've said worse to others, of course, and I love a bit of chat. I don't mind people giving it to me. It's fun. I enjoy it.

Not once did I hear the English say 'Mind the windows' to me after that. I bowl so quick that they're probably scared of me! I get more sledging in club cricket in Barbados about it than in international cricket. That's because the Barbadians are all super-talented and not afraid of you. They tell you what they want to tell you. They love hooking and pulling, as it's what they're brought up doing. It all comes through the no-fear mentality of tape-ball cricket.

And, if Freddie got me that time, which they say he did, I got him in the Caribbean. It's Freddie one, Tino one. The great man will admit that himself too.

We were playing in Trinidad in March 2004 and I'd just bowled over Nasser Hussain in my third Test match. He made fifty eight in nearly six hours when I knocked out his stumps. I was walking back to my bowling mark when I looked at mid-on and mid-off and neither of them had the ball. Then I saw it in umpire Daryl Harper's pocket. He still had it. I thought, 'Let's have some fun right here.' So I charged in like a man possessed. I was holding my fingers like I had the ball. I launched into my delivery to bowl and Freddie ducked. He didn't see it – because I didn't bowl it! He doesn't know where the ball is; he doesn't know what's happening. Then he realised I didn't have the ball. He pointed the bat at me, like, 'You prick. What are you doing?'

The whole of Trinidad was laughing. The place was rocking. Everyone on the field was in hysterics – except Fred. He was fuming. So I got him then, he got me at Lord's. There it is: one-all.

The captain that day was Brian Lara. Even he found it funny. He said, 'Tino, you are something else!' We were in the heat of a battle and all I wanted to do was make people laugh. Everyone was just so intense and I just felt like saying, 'Calm down, boys. Let's smile.'

Two years after I bluffed Fred with the ball, I was talking with the great man Sachin Tendulkar and he told me it was the funniest thing he'd seen in his life. If the legend that is Sachin Tendulkar is having a conversation about it, I'm happy. At least I made a legend laugh.

Despite being made to look a fool, I love England. My great-grandfather always said I'd have played eighty or ninety Test matches if I was English. He used to say I needed the right coaching and that I would have got it in England. He's my mother's grandfather: Ulrich St A Reid. He emigrated from Barbados to England in 1956. I don't know if he was right – I think ninety was maybe a bit too many – but I would have got a better run. The structure in England is just so much better; so much more professional. You can play county cricket in England for twenty years and take home a decent wage and live a really good life. If you don't play for the West Indies, you'll be working nine-to-five back home.

I didn't see my great-grandfather as much as others may see their family because he was 4,000 miles away. But as a kid growing up, and still now, we are close. When I come over to England, I'll live with him in Thornton Heath, near Croydon in London and help him with his food and little chores around the house. We'll sit for an hour a day chatting away too.

He used to write me letters addressed to 'Master Tino la Bertram Best' when I was young. Man, it made me feel proud. I used to take the letters into school to show my teachers. 'Look, he called me master – I am a master,' I used to say. Everyone would laugh as I showed them but I didn't care: I felt so proud. Here was a wise man in England, writing to me to talk about cricket. He'd talk about life, send me pictures and discuss me becoming a champion. When he came to Barbados to see us, I would follow him every day. I just loved spending time with him. My father wasn't there but this great-grandfather was exactly that: great.

But despite my great-grandfather's beliefs that I would have been an English star, I was very much West Indian. It was my dream, after all, to go out and open the batting for the West Indies and make a load of runs against teams like England.

I played six Test matches against England: four in the Caribbean and two over there. The first came in 2004, when I took my first Test wicket at Sabina Park. Graham Thorpe, the man. What a moment that was. He'd seen me playing as a thirteen-year-old kid in 1994 on the outfield at the Kensington Oval and was impressed. I was there with Dario Haynes, Desmond Haynes' son, and Carl Greenidge, Gordon Greenidge's son. We were the three musketeers who all wanted to follow our family path to play for the West Indies. Haynes and Best: the two West Indian batsmen. Jason Lloyd, Clive Lloyd's son, used to knock around with us too sometimes. Lloyd and Greenidge wanted to be the great West Indian bowlers. These were our big dreams as kids.

Thorpey gave me his bat – his Kookaburra – and I told him it was my dream to open the batting for the West Indies. Then years later he became the first man I dismissed. It was crazy. That's probably the second best moment of my career. I'll tell you the other later.

Devon Malcolm gave me a bat that same year and I struck up a really good relationship with him. I may have been nine years old but I wasn't short of a word or two. 'I'm going to hit you round the park,' I used to tell him. Then I'd rub salt in the wounds and remind him, 'Just like my Uncle Carlisle did!' He's a great man and we're still in touch.

Alec Stewart was a great of that era too. He saw me playing in 1994 when England toured the Caribbean and asked who my father was. When I told him that my family connection came through my Uncle

Carlisle, he was so excited. Carlisle Alonza Best: the legendary batsman who commentated while he batted. He was causing excitement even after his Test career was over. I told him Uncle Carlisle was working in a bank and Alec passed on his best wishes.

After the Freddie jibe, I had to wait eight years until I played against England again. Bad coaches, baffling selections, back-crunching injuries – I suffered with the lot. I was in the one-day squad but I just didn't get put in the Test side. To this day, I still don't know why. The West Indies selection criteria is strange now. I enjoyed one-day cricket like I enjoyed all cricket but I wouldn't say I was more suited to it in any way. But they wanted me for the shorter form, not the longer form. I guess it was horses for courses but I don't know why this was in my case.

In 2012 I sat on the bench for an entire one-day series against Australia in the Caribbean. We did OK, drawing 2-2, but I was so disappointed I didn't get to play. I was thirty, at the peak of my powers, but I had to watch from the sidelines. I'd been working hard but the team were playing decent cricket.

We had Kemar Roach in the side: a real talent with express pace. He could be absolutely fantastic for the West Indies if he stays fit and playing. Andre Russell was ahead of me too. He's a bowling all-rounder and a big talent in limited overs cricket. He's played in the Indian Premier League and you don't get there without having serious ability. Then there was Ravi Rampaul: a real seasoned player who had been bowling really well at the time. He was one of the West Indies' best one-day bowlers so it wasn't easy to break into the side.

After that one-day series, the team went over to England. I wasn't in the Test squad, so I went back home to Barbados. As part of my deal as a Barbados player, the Barbados Cricket Association got us to do some coaching work with the youngsters at the Kensington Oval. I was working with the Under-13 team on a Monday night, imparting some knowledge, which I love doing. I love to inspire the next generation.

I watched the first Test at Lord's and it hurt. Eight years earlier, in 2004, I'd been steaming in, bowling at the speed of sound. But here I was, watching the TV with no idea why I wasn't playing.

That night, down at the Kensington Oval, Courtney Browne came over and offered me his congratulations. I had been recalled – not that I'd heard. Shannon Gabriel had gone down with a back injury during the first Test. Lord's was his debut and he started well, taking four wickets. But he didn't bowl after lunch on the final day because he had some kind of stress reaction in the lower spine.

Back from the wilderness, I was soon packing to come to England. What the frig? Where's this come from? There were only three Tests. I didn't get to play in the second at Trent Bridge but I did get my chance in the third Test at Edgbaston. From coaching some under-13s, to playing against the English in Test match number fifteen of my career. Woah.

Unfortunately for Kemar, he got injured, so I was thrown into the final XI. I hadn't played Test cricket in three years. I woke up thinking, 'I'm really going to bowl quickly.' I thought about taking wickets; about getting a five-for. I wasn't thinking about batting. I was thinking about how I would hit KP on the pads, or nick Graeme Swann off – that kind of visualisation. But we were put into bat and the coach, Ottis Gibson, told me I'd be in at eleven. I told him I thought I should be batting at nine but he was having none of it. Sunil Narine was making his debut, on the back of tearing up the IPL, and he was in at nine. Ravi Rampaul was in at ten. Two left-handers, they were, who could bat a little bit. The boy who dreamed of opening the batting for the West Indies was in at eleven.

Narine walked to the crease, stayed around a bit and made eleven before he was bowled by Graham Onions. Then Ravi Rampaul came and went for two, caught by wicket-keeper Matt Prior, bowled by the paceman Steven Finn for two. Throughout all this, Denesh

Ramdin remained at the other end. He was well-set when I came in, on 60-odd, and we were 283 for nine. Ottis Gibson told me, 'Bobski, all I need from you is twenty five runs. Get us to 325. Hang in with Ramdin.'

I walked out and I just felt something different, almost supernatural. I felt I was just so good, that I had the chance to express myself. I had made my debut twelve years ago. It was almost as if this was my second coming. It didn't matter if I failed: I could just play with freedom and without any pressure. Onions was steaming in and I played a big booming drive to the third ball and missed. Even then, I felt good, almost as if it was an awesome play and miss. I played straight and it swung away from my bat. Well bowled.

I told Ramdin that, if anything was bowled in my half, I'd smoke it. I was seeing the ball so big. I had felt like that only once before: the fifty I scored when I was twelve, for Garrison School, against an under-15 side. That was the only other time I was seeing the ball like this. I was just so focused, so free of mind, with no pressure whatsoever. I told Denesh I'd stay with him and his instructions were to keep my head down and not burn out.

Graham Onions, Steven Finn, Tim Bresnan, Graeme Swann – they were all coming at me. And you know what? If I nicked off, it didn't matter. I was just so happy to be playing international cricket again. My whole life, people were telling me I would be the next Malcolm Marshall. 'You're short like him,' they said. I had a lot of pressure on me and that's never easy to deal with, being in that kind of environment. I always tried to do the best I could but I'm not Malcolm Marshall. I'm Tino Best and this was the chance for me to show people what I could do.

Before that series, I'd been watching *Fire in Babylon*, the film about the record-breaking West Indies cricket team of the 1970s and 1980s. It won awards, that film. It was something special. Colin Croft, Joel Garner, Gordon Greenidge, Desmond Haynes,

Michael Holding, Clive Lloyd, Viv Richards and Andy Roberts all featured. All legends, those eight. This was my inspiration. It put my mindset right. I was in the West Indies team and I had to showcase my talent. It gave me a sense of belief and relief to play my game freely, to enjoy it and not carry the stigma of being the next Malcolm Marshall. That film freed my mind to just be Tino; to just be myself.

I was feeling good and I knew I could play. I think I can bat, I really do. I look at the players around now and I see they're classified as all-rounders. I feel like I could have been a genuine all-rounder for the West Indies. I told myself I wasn't going to swipe and to just play proper cricket shots. I backed myself and Ramdin backed me. 'You can bat. You were a batsman, buddy,' he said. I knew it and I told him to make a hundred for his wife. He made his debut in 2005 and I'd played a lot of cricket with him. I respect him a lot.

Denesh nudged his way to a hundred and I was made up for him. At the other end, I was going some. There was Graham Onions, a very clever bowler. Now I've always rated him and I think he was born at the wrong time. He played nine Tests for England but could have played many more. Bresnan and Swann were quality cricketers too. If you're a bits and pieces player, you may play one game before you're sussed out but these two were class acts.

I knew Bresnan well from my spell at Yorkshire. As for Swanny, I absolutely love him. He's the most gifted off-spinner of his generation. Everyone says they love Shane Warne and that he's the greatest. OK, Warney is the Michael Jordan of bowling but Swanny was absolutely fantastic: my favourite. He had a real natural action in a time where there were lots of spinners getting reported for theirs.

Swanny was bowling at me and he likes a word or two. Except it was me sledging him. I played a back-foot punch off him for four and loved it. Graeme Swann, 200-odd Test wickets and I'm just having a go. 'You can't get me out!' I said, laughing at him. 'I've hit Murali for four fours in a row and I'll murder this.' Matt Prior was behind the stumps and he couldn't believe it. He was calling me a crazy man, a nutter, and laughing with me. Prior was saying, 'Come on Swanny,' and I just turned round and said, 'Matt, he can't get me out here. For a case of Banks's beers, he can't bowl me out.' I was sledging Bresnan too. I hit him over his head for six. He turned round and said, 'Why didn't you bat like this for Yorkshire?' I laughed and told him, 'I'm going to cream you today.'

For two hours I was out in the middle and it felt like playing against the big guys in the village again. The sun was out – it was like being back home. I was showing the world what I could do. I felt like a youngster again.

I moved to fifty and it was pure jubilation. The crowd were on their feet and I had another surge of energy. The little kid from Richmond Gap was smacking around the English. There was a big West Indian contingent in one section of the stands and I jumped up and punched my fist to them. I looked up to the balcony and all my team-mates were there applauding me. Darren Sammy was standing at the front of them leading the reception. They knew I could bat – but they didn't know I could do this.

Past fifty, I didn't stop, past sixty, seventy, eighty and then ninety. It was all a blur of freedom. The only time anything other than watching the ball came into my head was when I moved on to ninety three. Malcolm Marshall's top score was ninety two. He was the man I was supposed to be. I remember thinking, 'Man, I've got on to ninety three. I've beaten the great man's best score.' Other than that, it was just a case of watch ball, hit ball. Easy. I got a two and three singles to go from ninety to ninety five. I thought to myself, 'You've been playing your shots. Hit one out the park to get to a hundred.' So I tried to do just that.

Onions came running in and I was ready – ready to smash it for six. He bowled a slower ball and I went to strike it over the leg-side but I top-edged it. The ball flew up in the air. Oh no, oh no.

Andrew Strauss was under it. Caught. Out for ninety five. Done by a slower ball. If it'd been pace, it'd have gone for six. I'm sure of it. There would be no hundred. The crowd were on their feet again. It reminded me of the Kensington Oval in 1990 when my uncle made 164. What a feeling.

People say to me, 'Tino, that was stupid. If you'd got five more singles, you'd have done it.' But no way: I don't play like that. I don't play cricket for the records. I enjoy the game and want to make people happy. I want to be spectacular. I want to be awesome. I could be like Geoffrey Boycott and bat all day and work the ball around. I could be like Chris Rogers and dig in and grind it out. But I want to be Tino Best, the great entertainer. I want to be like Glenn Maxwell or Chris Gayle. Cricketers should be bigger than life.

There's a certain aura about being flamboyant, showing your shots and inspiring people. There's a place for consolidating and working round: that's cricket. But I am West Indian and I will be flamboyant. If I'm on ninety nine, I'll try and hit a boundary to get to a hundred. It's just how I think the game should be played.

People say I must be gutted. No, I'm grateful I got to ninety five. It was two hours of pure fun. I nearly hit a hundred in a session and I was a number eleven – that's crazy. Credit to the England lads. KP came up to me and told me it was awesome to watch. Ian Bell, who I have a lot of time for and think is a really good batter, said something similar. Jonathan Trott couldn't believe it. 'Man, do you know how talented you are?' he said. 'You should just chill and take it easy. Your hand-eye co-ordination is awesome. But chill, man, you're too angry!'

Walking off that field on 10 June 2012, I felt like a youngster again. I showed the world what I could do. The kid from the village had played like he was back in his village. There was still time to bowl after that. I charged in and got Andrew Strauss, caught by Darren Bravo at slip for seventeen. I bowled over Jonny Bairstow too, another guy I played with at Yorkshire. I used to tell him, 'Jonny, any time we play international cricket I know how to get you out.' Bowl short balls, then get him on a good length. Don't get me wrong: he's pure class, is Jonny, but I knew how to get him out.

At the close of play, I felt very emotional. I got back to my hotel and just dropped to my knees with exhaustion. I thanked God for making it an awesome day. I couldn't believe I had made ninety-odd in a Test match. I was grateful for that, not dwelling on the fact that I could have got a ton. I turned on my phone and it crashed. There were so many messages from friends, family and on Twitter. Tino Best was the number-one trending topic in Europe. Madness!

My uncle messaged me but, always a perfectionist, he berated me. Still, I knew my family were proud. The most touching message came from my son Tamani. He rang me, crying. 'Dad,' he said, 'I can't believe you got out on ninety five.' I told him the only tears should be tears of joy because you should never be greedy. Then I said, 'Son, you will get your chance to play for the West Indies and you will score more than me. Your uncle struck a hundred and sixty four against England, Dad scored ninety five, you can score more than us both. You can make a double century.' Hopefully, he can do just that one day.

At the time, my ninety five was the highest ever score by a number eleven. Zaheer Khan scored seventy five against Bangladesh in 2004 and my knock beat his. But my record didn't last long. A year later, in July 2013, Australia's Ashton Agar scored ninety eight against England on his debut. He was a teenager at the time – a wonderful talent – playing in the first Ashes Test. He was in for his left-arm spin but, man, he could bat. The thing is that he was a number six, not a number eleven. That innings doesn't count in my book!

Denesh Ramdin thanked me for talking him right through to a hundred and I was happy for him. He was under a lot of pressure at the time. He'd scored fifty one runs in the first two Tests of that series – he made scores of one, forty three, six and one – and had been criticised for his glovework. But when he got to his century, he did something I didn't agree with.

He pulled a note out of his pocket and held it up. 'YEA VIV TALK NAH,' it read. I couldn't believe it. I was taken aback. He was having a go at Sir Viv Richards, a West Indies legend. I was embarrassed – totally embarrassed. In fact, it was one of the most embarrassing moments of my life. I had no idea he was going to do that and all I could think was, 'Don't, man. Don't.' I couldn't believe he would do that to a cricketing god. Sir Viv was working in the media and had every right to say what he saw. If Sir Viv had said he didn't think I was bowling well, there's no way I would get a five-wicket haul and start taunting him. The older you get, the wiser you get but you just never, ever take a shot at legends.

I don't know if Denesh regrets it. He's a decent boy and not a troublesome person at all. To be honest, he's a wonderful person. Sometimes we do silly things and maybe that was one of them. Sir Viv was doing his job. He's paid his dues too. He is one of the top-five greatest cricketers who has ever lived. He has every right to say anything about any cricketer he sees on the park. Denesh apologised to Sir Viv and he did the right thing there. You can't take the criticism to heart.

But what a day. I helped Denesh make a hundred and I made ninety five as well. Despite what Uncle Carlisle may have said, what was great about that knock was that it gave the family pride. I was on the back pages of the paper and everyone was talking about how good it was. I was a dad, a son, a nephew, a grandson and a great-grandson and I'd done the family proud. It gave a sense of achievement to them. They could go into work and say, 'Did you see the ninety five from Tino? That's my nephew.'

So, if you're telling me to mind the windows, remember to mind my ninety five too!

CHAPTER TWELVE

THE DOOMED REIGN OF A KING

I've played under some great coaches: Henderson Springer is one, Gus Logie another and Ottis Gibson is top notch too. But there's one of them I'll never forget – Bennett King.

I'll tell you now: I don't think Bennett King had a clue. He was appointed to replace Gus in 2004, just a few weeks after we'd won the Champions Trophy under his leadership. Bad move. Gus's Test record wasn't great – he won only four of twenty two Tests – but we were a good and improving side in ODIs. We'd won twenty out of thirty ODI games – a decent record – but, after winning the tournament, Gus had his contract terminated early. I was dumbfounded.

During the Champions Trophy, which I missed through injury, we'd beaten the best in the world and, thanks to two of my Barbados mates, we'd pulled off a miracle chase in the final against England. At 147-8, chasing 217 at The Oval, it was game over. Except Courtney Browne and Ian Bradshaw had other ideas. I'd left Tamani, who was just coming up to his fourth birthday, downstairs to watch the cricket while I lay in bed. I was in such pain with my back that I just had to sleep it off.

An hour or so later, Tamani was knocking at my door saying West Indies had won. What the frig? He was a kid but, even then, he knew how cricket worked. I wasn't totally surprised that Browne and Bradshaw had done it though. I've played all my life with those guys and it was just a Bajan thing. They went out there like it was a normal day at the Kensington Oval, backed themselves and the two close mates brought us home in the near dark. Brilliant for them and brilliant for Gus.

Gus understood the culture of the West Indies. He was tapping into our true potential and he knew what each player was capable of at each particular time. I was upset that Gus was treated like that and the way he was discarded as coach hurt me badly. Then, from nowhere, we had a new coach who I'd never heard of.

I missed the first few months of the Bennett King reign through the injury I sustained at Lord's. I was having physio every day and it was a gruelling test, both physically and mentally. I used to go to into schools to talk to kids about cricket and fitness and all I wanted was to be a good role model. It'd help me pass the time too but the whole thing left me so frustrated. At least I had my big return to look forward to.

A bit of research showed me Bennett King had coached Queensland, winning a few four-day competitions, and was leaving his job at the Australian Cricket Academy to take charge of us. He used to teach PE and had played first-grade cricket – but nothing more. I'm not saying you have to have played international cricket to be an international coach but it does help.

I played two first-class matches for Barbados in March 2005 before I was called back into the squad to face South Africa in the fourth Test. My second comeback game, against Trinidad, hadn't gone well. I pulled up after sixteen balls and didn't bowl again in the match. My back started stiffening out on me and they said they wanted me for the Test so I had to rest it up. They wrapped me up in cotton wool, even though we were 2–0 down and the lead was unassailable. It was the first decision that I disagreed with.

What greeted me in that camp was ridiculous. Bennett King was coach and David Moore was his assistant coach. But I use the word 'coach' in the loosest of terms – they weren't coaches. They were more like taskmasters. They came in and their thing was that West Indies players were lazy. So they set about grinding us to the ground with fitness work, day in, day out.

Now, I'm a fit person. I lived in the gym – I still live in there now – and I have a military background that kept me fit and strong. The need to be in the best physical shape was ingrained in me from a young age, yet, after that first spell in my first Test match on my return, I was tired. How was that possible? There were twenty wickets to take and the quick, strike bowler is knackered. How is that right?

King and Moore's training wasn't training. This was foolishness. They thought that, because we were flamboyant, we didn't try hard. Bollocks. Under King, we were forever doing a fitness test called the Malcom. You'd start on your stomach, get up and sprint, then get back on your stomach, sprint again and so on. We'd be ready to play Pakistan and Australia and the guys would be laughing at us and saying how unnecessary it was. I'd be thinking exactly that but I knew that, if I said something, I'd be kicked off the team. One thing that really freaked me out is that some Australia players said to me they'd played under King with Queensland and that he'd never got them to do that before. We'd do netting but they'd just overbowl us, so it was pointless.

I'm a big believer in having a coach that you trust and believe in and want to play for but in my opinion King and Moore were overdoing it. Shiv Chanderpaul was captain at that stage, having taken over from Brian, who was clearly upset. The mere fact we were training so hard was getting him down. At one stage, Brian said his arms were so sore that he couldn't lift a bat up. We're talking here about one of the best players ever to have played the game.

There wasn't any bad energy between the players because we were so united in our feelings. King and Moore worked us into the ground and everyone used to be tired before every Test match. I'm no stranger to working my arse off but not like this. This was overdoing it. I remember Brian, with his tired arms, ended up saying he wouldn't do this or that. He just picked what he wanted to do. He was a senior guy – a legend – but, at twenty three or twenty four, I didn't have much say in anything. I just had to do it.

In 2005, against South Africa, King put on West Indies whites and started taking water round the ground. The crowd at the Kensington Oval booed him. They were outraged that he was wearing West Indies gear. It was almost sacrilegious for them. I salute and applaud those West Indies fans. Well done, them.

A coach is supposed to push you even harder. You don't need any motivation to play international cricket but they should be on hand to make fine tweaks and get the best out of your qualities. King was more of a person to yell at you though. In one Test, he said to Pedro Collins, 'Why are you not swinging the ball?' Pedro said the ball wasn't swinging. The reply from King was, 'You've been picked to swing the fucking ball, so swing it.' Not exactly productive.

Before the fourth Test against South Africa, when I was recalled, he tried to make me bowl with a remodelled action. He was intent on trying to get me to bowl like his fellow Aussie Brett Lee. He wanted to make me a biomechanical bowler. Now, I love Brett Lee but I can't just go and bowl like him. It was a complete waste of time.

I didn't want to play for the coaches, which was a huge problem. Fortunately, I had the West Indian people to play for. We drew that Test, with Chris Gayle hitting 317 on his own. That merely served to paper over the cracks. Before the game, we'd been given a fitness test: forty-odd sprints in the middle of a series. This was brutalisation; this was just hell. I flew into Antigua for the game and my body was just tired. It was a massive shock to the system after the back injury I'd just had.

I got AB de Villiers out twice but I didn't feel strong with the new action. Ian Bishop told me it'd take time but screw that. A year ago Wayne Daniel was remodelling my action and I was lightning quick. I didn't need to make another change.

I snapped at Bennett soon after and said I wasn't going to bowl like that anymore. I want to bowl the way Wayne Daniel had taught me. I'd just had my action remodelled: I wasn't going to have it remodelled again. 'If you don't want to pick me, don't pick me,' I said.

I bumped into Courtney Walsh and he was supporting me. He told me not to let this Australian guy get into my head and to keep doing what I was doing. The only change I should make, he said, was to strengthen my abs. That was the reason he thought I'd got a stress fracture in England, because I'd played so much cricket and my abs had become weaker. He was right. I've done dead lifts three times a week since 2005 and I've not had a single back problem since. You couldn't tell that to Bennett King though. It's either the Bennett King way or the highway.

I'd had warning signs of what it might be like. I was watching one of the earlier Tests against South Africa when Reon King bowled Graeme Smith off a no-ball just before lunch. When he came off the field, Bennett was standing there with a tape measure. He stopped Reon going in and told him to go back out and mark his run-up again. Are you kidding me? I was watching at home and it incensed me so much. No one does that. It's just so disrespectful.

The bowlers used to complain about things a lot more than the batsmen, as they were feeling it more physically. Even Corey Collymore struggled under Bennett King. Corey was one of those very serious guys who went about his business very professionally. King picked up on that and, when Corey said he wasn't feeling in a good place and that he didn't feel like doing something, he was never pushed.

But it took time for Bennett to learn his lesson with Corey. Once he yelled at him so bad and Corey turned round and put him in his place. From that day on, he learned never to mess with Corey.

I was back in to face Pakistan in the second Test of the next series and I figured that was because Shiv demanded that we needed extra pace and power. I really found my groove in the second innings, taking four for forty six, my best bowling figures in Test cricket at that point. It all came when I was bowling with my Wayne Daniel action. Screw the Australian way.

I was on a high then, despite all my differences with King. Yet, instead of being rested and wrapped in cotton wool, I was sent on the A-team tour. He suggested I needed more bowling before I joined up with the senior team but that just left me feeling unwanted.

If there were problems with me and King, there were even bigger problems elsewhere. The senior team had a five-week tour of Sri Lanka to come but it was marred by off-field wrangles. The West Indies Cricket Board (WICB) and West Indies Players' Association (WIPA) were at war over a clause in a contract that covered players' individual endorsements and central team sponsorships. To be honest, it all got a bit messy. Was I interested in all this? No. Did I want to play for the West Indies? Yes. I just blocked it out and retained my focus: representing the West Indies.

Daren Ganga was the captain of the A-team and he told us the situation. He'd been talking to Dinanath Ramnarine, the executive president of the WIPA, and he wanted all the A-team players to boycott the full tour. If everyone said they wouldn't play, they'd have no Test series. While it was the WIPA's intention to get the series on, they wanted to protect the members' rights and interests.

I listened to all the chat and it didn't feel right. I didn't mind supporting the WIPA at all but I didn't have any retainer contract from the board. I had to pay bills and I did that by playing cricket. Brian Lara, Chris Gayle, Ramnaresh Sarwan and Fidel Edwards, among others, all sat out and missed the tour. They were all senior guys and they'd earned the right to do whatever they felt was right. I'm not saying they were wrong to do so but I play the game because I love it. The superstars were superstars and they'd been in the system for far longer than me. If they had a discrepancy, they had every right to air it, especially given what they'd done for West Indies cricket. I was just a small fish.

I stood up and said I'd play for free but that didn't go down well with Ganga. It was all pretty uncomfortable and sometimes I just wanted to disappear under a rock and hide. Playing for West Indies was all I wanted to do. Cricket is about cricket and the players should focus on playing. Let the administrators worry about the admin. I'm in love with the game, not the money. I love the West Indies and I'd happily play for nothing. From the moment I saw my uncle score a hundred against England, I fell in love with the game.

I wanted people to love me and watch me showcase my talent. It's the reason I'm still in love with cricket now. The greatest feeling ever is performing on the biggest stage. It's far better than having sex with beautiful girls or banking a load of money. Chris Gayle has played around the world and done everything. He will tell you there is no greater feeling than scoring 100 and playing in front of 70,000 people. It gives you a sensation you can't describe. If I was offered all the money in the world, I would resist it for a five-for against Australia on the Boxing Day Test match. You could hand me $1.5 billion, or give me Bill Gates' chequebook, and I'd say no. That or five for twenty eight against the Aussies? I'd take the five for twenty eight every time. I love cricket. She's my baby.

The series took on more importance given the situation in Sri Lanka. It was the first Test series to be played on the island since the devastating tsunami in 2004. The first Test at the Sinhalese Sports Club would also mark Sri Lanka's 150th Test, while Muttiah Muralitharan was returning after an 11-month absence through injury. It'd also be Tom Moody's first series as coach.

Of the more established players, Chanderpaul, Daren Powell and rookie Denesh Ramdin all committed to the tour before other A-team players followed my example in saying they'd play. We were nowhere near our best but we were there, playing for the West Indies.

In the press, Shiv was upbeat, saying, 'We have a group of young, new and exciting players like Xavier Marshall, Ryan Ramdass, Narasingh Deonarine and Tino Best who are keen and ready to play Test cricket. I know they are capable of doing the job. This is a good opportunity for them to make a name for themselves. I don't have much to worry about.'

Shiv was very quiet as captain. That's just how he was as a person. He was naturally a very humble and quiet man. He's one of those guys where you know what your role is: you're paid to do something you love and he expects you to go out and perform and do it. That's fine with me. I liked him, just like I loved most people deep down who played for the West Indies, even if sometimes it had felt lonely.

Shiv didn't have to play this series but he stayed because he loved the game. I wanted to make a name for myself and so did the others but, despite being a whole new group of players, many of whom were debutants, it was same old, same old for our coach Bennett King. He carried on grinding us into the ground. He even made Ryan Ramdass, who had played just one Test, cry. King made him run so many laps of the outfield that he couldn't take it anymore and broke down. He still seemed intent on killing us before the Test matches.

We lost the series 2–0 but we didn't do badly with that team. It was certainly no cakewalk for Sri Lanka. We had so many debutants that series that I think we won a few hearts with how we played – but not Bennett King's. After the match, he and his trainer, Bryce Cavanagh, had us doing sprints and more Malcom drills. Jermaine Lawson and I had been bowling against the classy Sri Lankan batsmen for days and we were knackered – but they made us do that. I asked the trainer what it was for. He said it was to make us fitter – but how can you be made fitter after playing five days of Test cricket? It just risks injury. You don't do sprints just because you've lost a Test match. I've been in the military – that's different. You don't play cricket for the West Indies to be punished.

On the pitch, I didn't have a bad time of it all in all. I smacked three fours in a row off Murali and he told me I should bat at three… I'll take that! Two of them were boomed through the covers and I walked down the pitch holding the pose on the second. I took three for fifty in the first Test too, including the wickets of Marvan Atapattu and Mahela Jayawardene. It certainly wasn't the worst performance in the world.

I was fined half of my match fee for bowling beamers during the second Test. They found me guilty of breaking the ICC's Code of Conduct, with Mike Procter, the match referee, ruling that my conduct was not 'within the spirit of the game'. What bollocks that was – it was totally unfair. I was trying to bowl a yorker at Murali, who was backing away. It came out full and it didn't even hit him. They weren't dangerous. They were full tosses outside off-stump. I explained myself but to no avail. It was a total mistake but they were having none of it.

In the one-day tri-series that followed, we even managed to beat a Sri Lanka team that included Sanath Jayasuriya, Kumar Sangakkara and Mahela Jayawardene. We fought really hard together and that's what I loved about it. It was actually one of the best tours I'd been on. We just enjoyed each others' company as a group.

The Sri Lankan people were brilliant, the hospitality was good and the hotels were real nice. I met a lovely young Swedish blonde too, which is always good, and enjoyed plenty of time with Dwayne

Smith, who was a bundle of laughs. A snake dropped out of a tree on him once and I'll never forget him running off screaming. We were just loving Sri Lanka.

When Gayle, Lara and co. did come back, I don't think they held the fact that I'd played in that series against me. They knew I was young and everyone wants to stand for what they want to. If you don't stand for something, you'll fall for anything. All I was doing was standing for my love: the game of cricket. Cricket had given me everything, so I wanted to play.

When the stars came back for the tour to Australia, we were far stronger. We played a practice game against Queensland and I took a wicket in each innings. I bounced Matthew Hayden out but I was happier with how I felt with ball in hand. I thought I was a quicker and stronger bowler than on my debut and I was far better equipped to do damage. At the time, Corey Collymore wasn't 100 per cent, Jermaine Lawson wasn't fully fit either, Daren Powell was struggling with his groin and Fidel was here or there. I was sure I'd be playing, as I was in fitter and in stronger shape than the rest of the bowlers. I'd just come from the Sri Lanka tour, where I'd been bowling really well too.

But, when the series started, they didn't start me. What more could I do? This coaching staff didn't rate me. We lost the series 3–0. There were warm-up games but I didn't give a frig. I didn't want to be out there just to be some kind of practice bowler. I was so pissed that the coaching staff weren't supporting me in what I wanted to achieve – so that was that. I just went out, partied, had sex with different girls and enjoyed my life.

That's where it reached boiling point. We were at the Allan Border Field in Brisbane and the Australian press wanted to do an interview with me. As I waited, I started juggling a football. I'm a big Chelsea fan, after all, and I wanted a couple of seconds thinking I was Didier Drogba. Then, from afar, I heard an almighty yell. David Moore was shouting at the top of his voice, 'Get your butt over here.' It sent me over the edge. I flipped and yelled back at him, 'Slavery has finished! You can't yell or shout at me! I'm not one of your kids.' I gave him a piece of my mind and I was sent back to the hotel. It'd never be the same after that.

Bennett King saw I was done later on that tour. He called me into a room, looked me in the eyes and told me, 'Trust me. I'm going to invest in you.' I was like, 'OK, cool, coach.' He was all ready to invest in me then. Except that was the last Test series I was involved in under him. Those guys were jokers. They tell a player aged twenty four, who's the quickest in the team, that they'll invest in him and then leave him out. I felt mugged off.

My last international game under Bennett King came against Zimbabwe in an ODI in Georgetown, in May 2006. I wasn't fully fit and I told him so. My hamstrings were hurting and I was far from 100 per cent. 'You guys are soft. This is Zimbabwe. Just run in and bowl because they'll be scared of you,' he said. I bowled ten overs – one for seventy – and I was in bits after. They were scared, were they? It didn't look like it to me.

I didn't like King and Moore and they didn't like me – they set me back three or four years. They robbed me of those years of my career. I had to play A-team cricket in England in 2006 after the Zimbabwe game. They said I needed to get more overs under my belt and to improve my fitness. Rubbish. My body was at breaking point and I couldn't take it anymore.

We played a one-day game against Worcestershire where we were chasing 306 and, at 152-2, we were cruising. But we relaxed, got beaten and it all came to a head. David Moore, Bennett's assistant who was in charge of the A-team, tore into us. Ryan Hinds got run out without facing and Moore turned and said, 'You got run out because you are fat.' Ryan snapped and said to Moore, 'You're fat too.' I lost it: this was fucking ridiculous, this was shit, it was crap. You can't call someone fat when you're out there yourself drinking Cokes every day. And that was me done – no more games under King.

Put simply, Bennett King and his coaching staff were a waste of time. The only good thing to come with them was Stephen Partridge, our Australian physiotherapist. He was the best physiotherapist I've ever come across. He was professionalism personified. The others weren't bad human beings, as such, but I don't think they had the right ideas. I wasn't alone in how I felt about the regime. The squad didn't appreciate them and didn't want them to be around. Every single cricketer in that West Indies team was tired. It didn't get me down as a person but it did affect my cricket.

I went back to Barbados and I appreciated it so much more after being left out the squads. I was way more loved by the Bajan boys. I liked the West Indies boys but those two coaches, King and Moore, nah. King resigned as West Indies coach after the team failed to reach the World Cup semi-finals in 2007 but I didn't care. I didn't even realise he'd gone, as I was way out the picture. I wasn't bothered about him anymore.

After King left, Ramnaresh Sarwan gave an interview to the *Jamaica Observer* newspaper, where he said, 'The coach was not as open as I would have liked and he was definitely not firm enough. He was also very aggressive and vocally abusive to certain players to the point where he even threatened them. Obviously, this made those players very uncomfortable.'

Well said, Ramnaresh.

CHAPTER THIRTEEN

YORKSHIRE... AND THE KID WITH A SMILE

It's cold, wet and 4,500 miles from home but I love Yorkshire. What a place – what a cricket club.

I was coming off the back of the ICC Champions Trophy in 2009 when I told my agent to get me to Yorkshire. There were two teams I wanted to play for as a boy: Surrey – because my grandparents came from there and I loved Mark Ramprakash – and Yorkshire.

It all came down to Darren Gough. He was one of my English heroes. Hendy (Henderson Springer) used to bring cricket tapes into the BDF Sports Programme and I was so in awe of Goughie. He was short, like me. He was stocky, like me. And he wanted to bowl quick, like me.

I remember seeing Gough bat against Australia at the Sydney Cricket Ground in 1995. He played so many shots and ended up making fifty one off fifty six balls. That was to be his second-highest Test score ever. Then I saw him come out and bowl super-quick, with a big smile on his face and with all the confidence in the world. I'd fallen in love with Darren Gough and I wanted to play for Yorkshire.

I was lucky enough to meet Darren in 2004 when he played for England in Barbados. He'd retired from Test cricket then and was only playing the one-dayers. He'd heard interviews of me talking about how much I adored him and we swapped jerseys. I was star-struck. Oh my God, Darren Gough, I couldn't believe it when we met. He was everything I expected him to be and more – and his energy was so infectious. Meeting him was so riveting and so surreal. That's one of the big reasons why I loved the Dazzler.

Yorkshire came to tour Barbados in 2010 and my agent sorted me to go down for a net session. I'd been dropped by the West Indies because all the big boys had come back in and they were fine for me to go down and practice.

I steamed in during that session and kept beating all the batters for pace. Steve Oldham, the Yorkshire bowling coach, called me over and asked what the problem was between me and Ottis Gibson, the West Indies coach at the time. There was no problem: it was just down to the selectors. They didn't want me.

Steve asked me what I thought about county cricket and, of course, I told him I'd love the opportunity to play and it all went from there. The coach, Martyn Moxon – or Frog, as we called him – said he wanted me to play in a two-day practice game against Lancashire, so I did. We were playing up at the 3Ws Oval, a decent ground in Barbados that hosts first-class cricket. It was eerily quiet, with just a few English tourists there to watch.

It was a real slow pitch that day but nothing could stop me. I was desperate to show I was good enough to be a Yorkie. I steamed in and bowled fourteen overs, eight of which were maidens, and took one for twelve. No one could lay a bat on me. I'd done enough to impress.

The other overseas player, Daryl Tuffey, had broken his hand and Frog asked me if I was keen to replace him at Yorkshire. Was I keen? This was Darren Gough's county. This was Chris Silverwood's county. This was Craig White's county, who I'd seen bowl at 90 mph and loved. Are you kidding? Of course I was keen. I wanted to play for Yorkshire and I wanted to play a part in their great cricketing history.

I was head over heels when I signed a contract there but sometimes things conspire against you. When I say things, I mean a volcano in Iceland. Over 100,000 flights were cancelled because the volcano erupted and an ash cloud swept across European airspace – and my flight was one of them. It meant my arrival was delayed for two weeks and I didn't get into the country until day one of the third game of the Championship season, against Kent.

We drew that game, after winning the first two, and I would make my debut in the Pro40 tournament against Essex, at Chelmsford. Alastair Cook, now the England captain and one of the country's best ever batsmen, was opening. Cookie's one of those guys who is a bit unorthodox, like Graeme Smith. He's not overly attacking but he has a very strong defence. He's someone who really digs in and fights for his runs.

There was a big crowd at Chelmsford, all shouting my name. They're supposed to be one of the more vocal and boisterous crowds in county cricket but they were cool with me. I overstepped in my first over and gifted Cook a free hit, which he smashed for four. Damn. Then I ran in, released a 95 mph missile and bowled him. What's more, that ball was so frigging fast that it snapped the stump in two.

I went mental, running in front of the pavilion to Froggy. That one's for you, Moxon. I took four for forty seven that day but I should have got seven wickets as I was bowling so quick. I'd had a good start and we'd won. Welcome to England.

Two days later we met Durham at Headingley: my first game on home soil. It started well as I took four for eighty six from twenty two overs. Ian Blackwell and Phil Mustard – who, between them, had played forty seven games for England – and Ben Stokes, the next big thing in English cricket, were among my victims.

The press were asking me about the pitch being slow afterwards but I wasn't too bothered. I was just happy to be at a ground that so many legends had played at. I told a reporter from ESPN Cricinfo, 'Friday is surfing day in Barbados but I'd rather be here playing cricket at this lovely ground. I thank God every day for giving me the talent to play cricket and I thank God for blessing Martyn [Moxon] with the insight to sign me for Yorkshire.' I meant every word.

The Yorkshire pitches were good. Headingley was a bit slow but the ball moved around a lot. The quickest pitch I played on was at Scarborough, against Essex, in my second County Championship game. The ground staff up there were awesome. I got a three-for in the first innings and Steve Patterson, at the other end, took five. Well, I say he got them – I reckon I got those five for him as the other batsmen didn't want to face me! It was his maiden five-wicket haul. He owes me for that.

Steve Patterson was one of my favourite blokes at the club. We used to call him Deadman because he had the deadest personality ever. But he's just brilliant and one of the hardest workers in county cricket, who deserves all the success he gets.

What struck me from day one was that the whole set-up at Yorkshire was just so professional. It's the most professional I've ever been involved with. We'd turn up wearing our blazers and ties to home games. I love looking the part – it was like being back at the BDF Sports Programme, getting yourself so nicely presented. On days off, we still had to report to Headingley with the rest of the lads. We'd eat breakfast, do fitness work, hit balls, train, do strength-and-conditioning work and eat our dinner together before we went home. It had an atmosphere like no other place in the world.

Aside from international cricket, the Roses game against Lancashire was one of the biggest matches I've played in. In terms of rivalry, it felt like a big Barbados versus Trinidad or a Barbados versus Guyana game at the Kensington Oval. Those are massive – and so is a Roses game. Headingley goes absolutely wild. I couldn't believe how intense it was. The verbal chat is so passionate as well; it's awesome. I absolutely love it.

I bowled a spell at Lancashire once in a game we drew. I took three for forty in the second innings to get them seven down before light intervened. I ripped through the top three: Paul Horton LBW, Stephen Moore bowled and Simon Katich, the Australian great, nicked off. To run in and see Katich edge one to Adil Rashid was amazing. It felt like Old Trafford went wild with all our guys' reactions. To be honest, I felt like I'd just nicked off Lara.

The two sets of players respected each other off the field but, when we crossed the line, it was a different story. Us Yorkies never liked the Lancs and the Lancs never liked the Yorkies. That was drummed into me from the moment I arrived in England. You hear the Yorkies say there's nothing ever good down the M62, the motorway linking the two counties. I got drawn into the cockiness of Yorkshire and I loved it. It was like living in Barbados. We had that attitude of 'we are the best and everyone else sucks'. It was a privilege to breathe the crispness and freshness of the Yorkshire air.

Our dressing room was so tight. It was like the Barbados dressing room I adored so much back home. The reception I got was good too. To hear Geoff Boycott, who scored 150 first-class 100s and 8,114 Test runs, say it was a pleasure to have me over made me so proud. To have those people respect me and even mention my name was something else.

While, over in Yorkshire, I came across two of the nicest young lads I've ever had the honour to meet. They were brothers: short lads, from Yorkshire, both batsmen, always wearing smiles.

There was one who just looked really solid. He was born to be a cricketer. The way his kit fitted him, the way he pulled his bag –

the boy was class personified. He had modelled himself on Michael Vaughan, who was a model citizen himself. He was young but there was this warm aura about him.

The pair of brothers worked so hard at their game. The elder one, looking the part and trying to be like Vaughany, used to tell me to go full pelt at him. He wanted me to crank it up in the nets and never give him a break. He didn't care if he got injured. He had balls.

That season, he played one of his first matches for the senior Yorkshire side against India A. They were all over us and had racked up 452-2, with Shikhar Dhawan and Ajinkya Rahane making 100s. I was steaming in, after hours of us all toiling away, when I got Rahane to nick one to slip.

The elder brother was there and he took the catch. He ran up to celebrate, grinning from ear to ear, telling me it was the fastest ball he'd ever caught in his life. The boy made me laugh and I knew then, after watching him in the nets and seeing his attitude, that this kid was going to be a star.

Good catch, Joe Root. And good luck, little bro Billy. He's now playing for Nottinghamshire.

Joe's such a sweet kid, even now. He really is the all-round package. He's aggressive, calm, brave and knows when to accelerate. He can play all forms of cricket and he's got a beautiful technique. He loves facing fast bowling and he's a class act against spin. Joe Root was hooking and cutting Mitchell Starc in the Ashes when he was bowling absolute rockets. Back in the day, the English players may have backed away – but not Joe. It just shows the culture at Yorkshire and their structure. It's brilliant. Put simply, Joe is a future England captain. He's going to score 12,000 Test runs too.

In truth, he was one of many at Yorkshire that impressed me. Jonny Bairstow and Adil Rashid were the same. They wanted to face me. I might hit them, I might break a rib, but they didn't care. They would stand their ground and that's the character of a Yorkshireman. That's why all three are so successful. They're all brave, with big balls. They all play for England now and it's all down to Martyn Moxon. He'd get the lads to be brave all the time. That's just how he wanted the guys to play their cricket – and it's just what was drummed into me by Henderson Springer when I joined the BDF Sports Programme at sixteen.

They say that, when Yorkshire cricket is strong, England cricket is strong. It's totally right. The same goes for Barbados and West Indies. If the Barbados team is going well, generally the West Indies will be too. I'd love to see a Yorkshire team take on an England team. It'd be a good game.

Jonny Bairstow and I were very close. We used to party together, with Adil Rashid, and I knew he had the ability to go places. He had a steely determination and an attitude of working really hard. He scored an amazing sixty four not out off sixty one balls against Warwickshire, late in the day, to win us a County Championship game. That knock showed what he was all about: he backed himself and he had confidence pouring out his ears.

What Martyn Moxon did with those youngsters was incredible. We had a little disagreement over me being dropped once but Frog is up there with the best three coaches I've ever had in my life. The thing about Frog is his eye contact. That's very important to players. He makes eye contact with you to make you believe in yourself. He's one of those guys who'd invite you round for dinner to make you feel at home. He's a strong man, not one to mess around, but always kind. His one main objective is to instil belief in you and he does that.

Of the coaches in the West Indies, Henderson Springer is the best of them, while Dexter Topping, who is second in command of the Barbados team, is not far behind. Springs and Moxon are very similar, imparting a hard-work ethic. Dexter is more of a yeller.

Moxon made the young boys at Yorkshire believe they were stars before they were stars. He saw that star quality in Joe Root and Jonny Bairstow before the world knew who they were.

The Yorkshire bowling coach, Steve Oldham, too, is a man who I have a lot of respect for. He made little tweaks in my action, getting me tighter and ensuring I kept my head still. When I came to Yorkshire, I was out the West Indies team and, after I left, I got back in. I was taking three-, four- and five-wicket hauls when I got back to Barbados and it came down to the work I'd done at Yorkshire. They helped me to be named as a reserve in the World Cup squad in 2011, when everyone felt I should have played. I'll always be grateful for that.

I was really impressed with Ajmal Shahzad when I was there. He made his Test match debut that summer and has played eleven ODIs and two Twenty20 internationals too. He should have been one of the best strike bowlers that England has had but I don't know what happened with him. He's extremely talented and he could swing the ball but he just didn't kick on. I think he's one that slipped through the net.

My spell wasn't without its run-ins. Of course it wasn't: it's high-stakes professional cricket. I had one particular one with Dominic Cork. I gave him a bouncer and he told me to keep on bouncing him. Challenge accepted. I told him I was going to cut him, I bowled a barrage of short balls and he gave me back talk. I got him out LBW in the end and I chased him off. At the end of the game, the umpires called us both in a room. They weren't happy. They told Dominic he was a former international cricketer, told me I was trying to get back in the West Indies team and that there shouldn't be any trouble. I accepted the ticking off and that was that. Me and Dominic are good friends to this day. The thing about cricket is that you have to leave it out on the field. It's nothing personal. It's just a game.

People say there's too much county cricket played but I'm not having it. In England you do really specific training in the off-season because you play so much during the season. In Barbados it's completely different. The English schedule is busy and you may be playing five or six days a week but the key is having a big squad and rotating it well. I love that you get to play so much. It feels like you're hardly ever playing cricket in the Caribbean but it's so different in England.

What I picked up from playing in England is how professional you have to be. My season in Yorkshire made me fitter, faster and stronger – and that's all down to the strength-and-conditioning coach Tom Summers. He's the man who helped me bowl so quickly. I learned stuff off him that I've taken with me in the rest of my career.

Off the pitch was good fun too. The guys at Yorkshire labelled me the biggest playboy going after an incident at Hampshire. We were playing a County Championship game down there when I saw a stunningly gorgeous girl. None of the guys could believe how beautiful she was. I said to them, 'Look, guys, I'll pull her by the end of the day.' They told me I had no chance; that I wasn't that good. But don't ever, ever challenge Tino Best.

I started to talk to her and she was mine in one. I pulled her, slept with her and had made a point to the lads. I came back and they told me I was the greatest puller of all time. The jiggy boss never loses.

In the end, a hamstring injury meant I had to go home early. So how do I think I did? I think I was a decent signing. I don't think I'm the worst signing ever, put it that way. If you look at other international cricketers, very few fast bowlers have been able to become accustomed to conditions in England straight away. South Africa's Dale Steyn struggled when he first came over to Essex, taking fourteen wickets at an average of sixty, and only found his form when he came to Warwickshire a few years later.

At Yorkshire I took eighteen County Championship wickets at forty four, ten one-day wickets at sixteen apiece and seven wickets in the Twenty20 Cup at thirty four, with an economy of just over eight. I helped them win plenty of one-day games as we topped our group, only to lose out to the eventual winners Warwickshire in the semi-finals. By that time, I was back home because of my hamstring. I love England and English people and would love to play in the County Championship again.

I could have taken more wickets but I enjoyed every one and at least each one gave me a chance to celebrate like Didier Drogba. I used to watch a lot of the English football Premiership when I was young in Barbados and I loved it. As a kid, I saw so much Dutch football and my team was Ajax. During the mid-1990s I saw Dennis Wise, Marcel Desailly and Jimmy Floyd Hasselbaink play, and Chelsea became my team. I'm Chelsea for life now. People love Cristiano Ronaldo and Lionel Messi but I used to idolise Drogba. So, when I got a wicket, I'd get the arms out the side and start jigging with it. He was the man.

I feel so blessed to have played for Yorkshire, to take wickets and help them come third in the Championship. To play at Headingley, to play at Scarborough, to be in the team that beat Essex in two and a half days there: I'll never forget that.

One thing I've always enjoyed about playing in England is that I've never got any stick: in county cricket or with the West Indies. All I've ever got was encouragement. I would come down to the crowd to sign autographs and they would tell me to bowl faster and knock the batsman's head off. At Headingley the DJ used to play 'Simply the Best' whenever I came on to bowl. Man, I loved it.

In Barbados, though, you get stick. I've heard people yell at me when I'm going up to bowl. I've been called all sorts – a 'bald-headed idiot' is one of my favourites. Other people told me I shouldn't have been playing for Barbados because I was no good. I've been shouted at when playing for the West Indies. Even when I've been playing club cricket, I've heard yells.

The Caribbean people just like to get stuck into you. I was over in England playing an exhibition game for Lashings – more about them later – in the summer of 2015. There was a Caribbean chap there watching, with the biggest gut I'd ever seen. The bloke was huge. Bear in mind that this was an exhibition game but he started shouting stuff from the boundary. He was getting stuck into me for being unwanted in the CPL. He said I was no good; he said I was the worst. I just turned round and smiled at him. Eventually, someone got so annoyed with him that they told him to give me a break.

At the end of the game, an English lady came up to me to chat. She said I'd gone up so high in her estimations for keeping my mouth shut and she called me a legend. It was so nice but I'm used to the barracking. That's the West Indian culture right there: they just love to criticise you.

But it wasn't all good. The saddest thing happened in Yorkshire. I was seeing this beautiful mixed-race girl named Lauren. Me and my boy Gerard Brophy met her after the Roses T20 game when we won and went out with all the boys. Lauren and I were dating and I was really fond of her. She was studying for a career in the public-health industry but fell back at uni and got depressed. She got into a rut and, in 2011, she took her own life. I rarely get hit out the ground – except then. That hit me for six. Rest in peace, Lauren.

My first experience of playing in England and enjoying the love of the people had come in 2002 with Madeley Cricket Club, a team who played in the Staffordshire League. They contacted the BDF Sports Programme and told them they wanted a pro. They had read about how quick I could bowl and asked for me to come over. I'd never played outside of Barbados and this was a wonderful opportunity to get away, learn new conditions, see what the cold weather was like and how the ball swings. I knew it'd be a whole new experience and I'd benefit hugely as a cricketer from it.

I wasn't scared of living away from home, as I'd done that for years with the BDF Sports Programme. That's what it prepares you to do. The programme paid for my accommodation and I took home £250 a game for myself. Happy days.

There were some fantastic people there. After touching down in England, I went and met Loll Woodhall, the captain of the first team, and the president of the club, Mr John Bailey. Both were brilliant human beings who made me feel so welcome.

I've always been lucky to have some brilliant women in my life and it was no different when I was in Madeley. I stayed with a beautiful old lady called Miss Simms. She was the mother of the scorer, Craig, and she made sure I was well fed, that the beds were clean and I that was comfortable in my new surroundings.

It went well on the pitch, even if it was a bit cold. The atmosphere, weather and the pitches took a lot of getting used to. I took four-for in the first game and bowled so quickly that I was told I'd kill someone in the league! I think other teams made sure the pitches were as slow as could be after that. I got one or two scores and a few more wickets before I got the call from the West Indies A team – and that was that. The Madeley guys joked that it was all down to them.

In 2004 I was back in England for the whole summer with the West Indies. 'Mind the windows,' and all that – and then I signed to play league cricket again in 2007. Although that didn't exactly go to plan…

Nasser Hussain's brother, Mel, had organised for me to go to play for a team in Essex called High Roding. Mel was good friends with my Uncle Carlisle and his club had paid for my plane ticket to come over. I got there on the Tuesday of that week, all set to get underway at the weekend, but it wasn't to be.

We were due to play Springfield but they told the league they were considering pulling out of the game because they feared for their players' safety. The league held an emergency meeting and they banned me before I'd even played! I had represented the West Indies in international cricket within the last year and, apparently, that meant I wasn't allowed. I'm sure it was because I was too quick.

In the end, I did get a chance in a team called Crompton, in the Central Lancashire League, thanks to a man called Gary Kershaw who came in to get me on board. Man, those pitches were quick. It wasn't a bad standard either. Roelof van der Merwe, who has played for South Africa and Holland, was a pro for one of the other sides. And I was filling in for Darren Sammy – a class act himself – after he was called up for the West Indies.

I reckon I must have bowled at 100 mph during my time there. It felt like it anyway. I broke stumps, I broke bails and I bloody loved it. The guys at Crompton loved it too. If they didn't like a batsman on the other team, they'd come from mid-on or mid-off and tell me to make sure I hurt him. It was all good rivalry but really competitive.

Our captain at Crompton was Simon Wright, a really good slipper. Now, he used to catch everything. I came over and couldn't believe how good he was: he was real class. During one game, I nicked a batsman off and he came down to high-five me but couldn't. He showed me his hand and there was a massive ball mark on it because it had hit him so hard!

The next time I was in England was in 2008, for Leek, a club in Stoke-on-Trent. They have had a few good overseas players in their time, with Ottis Gibson and Albie Morkel both having played there. It started off great. For the first couple of games, I bowled real quick, took wickets and scored runs.

We played Imran Tahir's team, Moddershall, and the lads were saying how good he was: a leg-spinner who could really spin it, they said. I told them not to worry and that I'd smoke him – and I did. I must have creamed him for five or six sixes in my half-century before taking four for twenty three to win us the game.

But in the next four or five games, it all got a bit funny. Every time I had a guy plumb, the umpires used to call me for no-balls. I used to nick a guy off and they'd say he hadn't hit it. The umpires used to be out for me and I didn't know why. I could tell, from the way I landed on the front crease, that they weren't no-balls.

I got frustrated and got into verbal disagreements. Then I was accused of bowling deliberate beamers. I didn't know what the umpires' problems were. Whatever they were, they pissed me off. I was way more fiery then. I could have beaten an umpire up there and then. I was full of rage. I don't know if I was bowling too quickly and they didn't like it because it put the players they knew in danger – but something was up.

There were a few hints of people mentioning racism around that time. Did I think they were being racist? No. Did I say anything racial? No. I was bowling fast at guys and I sent down a few full tosses by accident. That's all. It wasn't dangerous. I wasn't trying to hurt people.

A guy at Leek said I had to go to a meeting because the umpires had complained. They said I was abusing them but I was just frustrated at the awful decision-making. The umpiring decisions only ever went against me and that used to get me even more wound up. I agreed with Leek that I'd leave, and that was that. After 63 overs, 11 maidens, 12 wickets for 279 runs, I was gone.

I didn't ever have a great time playing competitive club cricket in England. That's not down to the teams I played for but their opponents. I never had anything to prove but it was different for the others. These guys are village cricketers and it's the beauty of the game that we all got to share a pitch. But they'd get really psyched up to face me and often it used to end pretty sourly. I played against a team once and I didn't bowl well. Then I found out the guys we played against had created some kind of hate page against me on Facebook. Seriously, why would you do that? I never replied to it and it got taken down by the Facebook administrators. People just loved to criticise me and my performance and I didn't like it. Some days, I turned up to play and just felt like I shouldn't be there because I didn't enjoy it.

I spent the rest of that summer in 2008 playing for the Lashings World XI, just like I had done in 2007. That was far more fun. Lashings, if you haven't heard of them, are the Harlem Globetrotters of cricket. Some of the best players ever to play the game have turned out for them: Richie Richardson, Brian Lara, Sachin Tendulkar, Muttiah Muralitharan, Sir Viv Richards, to name a few.

The club is the brainchild of a businessman by the name of David Folb, who made his money in investments. Folby couldn't get into his local team and said he'd bring his own cricket team to play them: Lashings. He came up with the ridiculously good idea of building up a team of superstars and said he'd pay an appearance fee to make sure he beat everyone.

Lashings go around the country playing club sides, who pay a fee for the team to arrive. They set up a marquee and sell corporate tables to have lunch at, we entertain, there's an auction of sporting memorabilia and then an exhibition game. Sometimes we have 2,000 or 3,000 people at games. It's one of the best experiences I've had in cricket, bar playing for the West Indies.

The kids are so into it, seeing all these international cricketers playing at their ground, and it's just so riveting. I have them running up to me saying, 'Oh my God, Tino Best. How can I bowl as fast as you?' I just feel so much love from the youngsters, talking to them about the game and just trying to inspire them. I will always love doing that.

I've met some incredible people at lunches. All the players are on different tables, so you talk to people you've never met before. They want to know about the Flintoff sledge, my fastest ball, the best batsman I've bowled at. You start off as strangers and then build a bond, talk about each other's families, aspirations and goals. Then I get home and I see I've got Twitter messages from them and we continue to communicate. It's amazing for cricket. You can be Christian, a Muslim, like Manchester United, hate Manchester United, be into cricket, rugby or tennis – but sport unites people.

I've had the good fortune to meet some amazing people through Lashings. Adam Hollioake is one of the most amazingly humble people I've ever met – and also one of the craziest! I've known Phil 'Daffy' DeFreitas and Devon Malcolm since I was about eight and it's great to play with them. I can talk to them about the game. Oh, and tease them. I've told them that, if I played for England, I'd have played more Tests than those two put together!

Lashings is a brotherhood of legends. To play against – and with – these guys is an amazing feeling. To be in that environment again, when many have retired from playing professional cricket, is electrifying. To have a legend like the great Gordon Greenidge overseeing us is incredible. To hear Gordon talk about the glory days of the West Indies feels so good. These guys, to me, are bigger than life. I hope I'll enjoy their company for years.

CHAPTER FOURTEEN

MY BIG MOUTH... AND MY BIG RETURN

A World Cup – the dream of all dreams. It's the biggest stage of them all, where the best on the planet are united in the fiercest of battles. The Aussies, the English, the Indians: all engaged in one huge fight. It's what sportsmen live for. It's why you get up at the crack of dawn and put your body through the mill, and its the thing that makes those sleepless nights worth it. One day, just one day, you'll have that chance to light up the world.

I'd always imagined playing in a World Cup for the West Indies. I'd missed out in 2007 and was absolutely gutted. I thought I'd at least make the provisional thirty but no. No chance this time and it'd be four years until the next.

When it came, I was in a good place. Shortly before Christmas in 2010, I got the present of all presents – a call-up to the thirty-man squad for the 2011 World Cup in India, Sri Lanka and Bangladesh. I'd played just one ODI in the previous four years but I was buzzing to be back. And I was bowling quick.

The call hadn't been handed to me on a plate. I'd taken the West Indies Cricket Board Cup – the 50-over competition – by storm. Only my Barbados team-mate Ryan Hinds had taken more wickets than me – and he bowled twice as many overs. I ended up with ten wickets, at an average of ten, and I felt like I was sending it down at 100 mph. Four of those scalps came in the final as I got the ball swinging round corners both ways.

We shot the Leeward Islands out for 139 in that one and the trophy looked to be ours, until Lionel Baker took five wickets to rip through us. We managed to get the scores level before Kemar Roach called me through for a suicide single, for which there was no need to run. I don't know what he was doing and that call cost us the cup. Still, at least we didn't lose it.

Anyhow, I was in as a bowler and I was made up. When I spoke about my call-up with reporters, I meant every word: 'I am elated to be in the thirty. My bowling has improved tremendously this year and I am happy the selectors still have me in their thoughts. It would mean everything to me to be selected to play for the West Indies in the World Cup and get back on the international scene.'

I was left out of the final fifteen but I wasn't too disheartened. I was named as one of three reserves alongside Kirk Edwards, an out-and-out batter, and Devon Thomas, a wicket-keeper. If a bowler broke down, I'd be in. And, as I found out, with Ian Bradshaw in the trial game that made my career, injuries happen.

When you're a reserve, it goes without saying that you have to be ready to take your chance. I wasn't – and it was all down to my big mouth.

With it being the first-class season back home, I'd been at Barbados training with the team's female fitness trainer. Except I didn't like what she was doing. It's all right training people for fitness but training us properly to be cricketers is a different game and I felt she wasn't doing things right. You have to train different athletes in specific ways and I had a go at her and told her exactly what I thought about the situation. Bad move.

She was upset – so upset that she went to the manager, who got me banned for a game for expressing my opinion. So, with me needing overs under my belt to impress, in case someone went down injured at the World Cup, I was banned. I sat out of the first game of the four-day competition – the one I really wanted to play in – against the England Lions. They were the England A-side, containing a few of my old Yorkshire team-mates, including Adam Lyth and Andrew Gale, and I had to miss out. I returned to play Jamaica but, when I came back into the team, I wasn't at my best. Talk about the worst timing ever.

Out at the World Cup, Dwayne Bravo had gone down injured against South Africa as we lost the first game. His knee problem would rule him out the whole tournament and a replacement was needed. Dwayne got through overs in his role as an all-rounder. They'd need a bowler, surely...

They did – but it wasn't me. They called up Devendra Bishoo, a leg-spinner who'd never played an international game. I'm a fan of Bishoo now and he deservedly won the ICC Emerging Player of the Year award for 2011. I could have won that same honour myself in 2004 but I lost out to Irfan Pathan.

Despite his talent, it hurt that they'd gone for someone who wasn't even on the reserve list – all because of my mouth. If I'd have kept my mouth shut, I'd have played in a World Cup. I'd have played in the England game, then the Jamaica game and I'd have been on a plane to link up with my country.

Why didn't I just speak to the coach? Why did I yell at the fitness trainer? Why didn't I just do what she said, then worry about how it should be done later?

I hate living by regrets. I don't usually do it but I had done things the wrong way and there isn't a bigger price to pay than missing out on a World Cup because of it. To play on a World Cup stage would have been brilliant; incredible. It'd never happen.

I'd been in and out of the fold before that. Life as a West Indian cricketer is never, ever simple. The problem, it seemed, was that issues were developing with Barbados too.

At the end of 2007 I played four trial games and I took two five-fors for them. Happy days. I was looking forward to making the team with one-day cricket now coming more and more into the schedule. The chairman of selectors at the time, Roddy Estwick, had other ideas. Instead, they selected Pedro Collins, Fidel Edwards and Corey Collymore as their seamers. I was fuming, so I rang Estwick up to demand answers. I wanted to know why I'd been left out when I knew I'd bowled better and he told me I was being looked at as a four-day player. I was so pissed. He was being very disrespectful to my talent.

I always felt that, after Courtney Browne left the Barbados set-up, I didn't get the respect I was due. I gave everything I had but they never showed me much respect. Courtney guided me when he was playing and everyone knew he was a legend. The fact that he was taking care of me left a lot of people jealous. People would say I was Courtney's favourite – I won't name them but they were people around cricket – and I think it hurt them.

By the time I came back from the Sri Lanka Test series in 2005, Courtney had retired. Some of my Bajan team-mates said then that I was hardly going to make the Barbados team but it was rubbish. The reason why Courtney took me under his wing in the first place is because he saw I could win matches for Barbados. He knew how to get the best out of me and he appreciated my talents. They clearly didn't.

In 2006 the Stanford 20/20 tournament was launched in the Caribbean. It was devised by a man named Allen Stanford, a billionaire who wanted to bring West Indian cricket to life – or so he said. The games were played at his own ground in Antigua: the Stanford Cricket Ground. I missed out in the first year, as I was on duty with the West Indies A in England. In a straight-knockout format, Barbados got beaten by Trinidad and Tobago in the last eight. Trinidad went on to make the final, only to go down to Guyana.

The second edition of the tournament ran in 2008 and I was selected. How does that make sense? I wasn't selected for Barbados's 50-over team during that time but I did get called into the 20/20 side. Madness. I could make the four-day team and the 20-over team but not the 50-over team? And I'd played ODI cricket for the West Indies too. I still can't get my head around that.

We started the tournament well and I loved every minute of the format. It was action-packed from ball one. We only set 103 against Dominica in the first game but Sulieman Benn cleaned out their top order to get us into the last eight. I went wicketless but three overs and one maiden for twelve runs was a handy return. Benny was awesome in the quarters too, taking two for four from four overs, including one maiden, as we beat Grenada by fifty four runs. Into the semi-finals – happy days.

Trinidad & Tobago were a real strong team to face in the semis, with a batting line-up including Lendl Simmons, Daren Ganga, Dwayne Bravo, Kieron Pollard and Denesh Ramdin. Their attack, meanwhile, was led by Merv Dillon, the man who blanked me on my Test debut. We got off to an awesome start with the ball, restricting them to 120, and I was more than happy with my 4 overs only going for 15.

But, with a place in the final at stake, we just froze. The game was one of the most disappointing I've ever played in. The batsmen just made a complete mess of it and it was all down to nerves. We fell five runs short with four wickets left. Criminal. The day after that, I left for the ICL, devastated that we'd blown a chance to win a trophy. It didn't get any easier seeing Trinidad rout Jamaica by nine wickets to win it.

The ICL, as wonderful as it was at the time, caused its own problems. I loved the cricket but, off the field, I was left with real issues to deal with. The tournament collapsed following the Mumbai bombings in late 2008 and I hadn't been properly paid. I had to chase and chase the cash every day and it was a real tough time. Eventually, I got most of it but not all.

At the same time, a girl I was dating broke up with me. We'd been together a while and we'd been getting on really well. She was really different to me in that I came from quite humble surroundings and she was well-off. She'd never been short of money and her family had high expectations of her. Times got real tough for me, what with being ditched by the West Indies, then not being paid properly for my stint in India, and she switched on me. She left me and I was cut up.

It was tough to get myself right for Barbados after that, with so much going on away from the game. We lost a one-day final to Trinidad – who else? – and we finished fifth in the four-day table. I managed to take twenty wickets in the four-day competition in 2009, at an average of twenty five, but it was far from a memorable time.

I wasn't the only one having contractual problems at that time. Just like in 2005 with Sri Lanka, in 2009 the WIPA and the WICB were at odds again in a long-standing row over retainer contracts for players. Chanderpaul stuck it out before and played but this time even he'd had enough as he joined Gayle, Sarwan and the rest in boycotting the visit of the Bangladeshis.

My big brother Floyd Reifer had last played a Test in 1999 but he was named captain of the 2009 side. Kraigg Brathwaite was just sixteen at the time but he'd been included in a fifteen-man party. He didn't play but it showed where we were at the time. Kraigg isn't the most talented batsman but he works hard at his strengths. He has the application to score 8,000 Test runs – just he's not your typical flamboyant West Indian batter.

And I was back. Despite having a bit of a season to forget, the West Indies cricket manager, Tony Howard, rang me six days before the

Test and asked me if I was fit and ready to play for the West Indies. You never turn down the chance to play for your country, so I was on the next plane down to St Vincent. The senior players had gone on strike but the tour must go on. For me, it was the perfect chance to get ahead of Lionel Baker in the West Indies pecking order and rejuvenate my career. I'd pull on the famous whites again.

But, if there was any hope of it being a dream comeback, it was quickly extinguished. Floyd is a good lad but he was way past his best at that point. He'll admit just that himself. It was an opportunity for him to make a mark on West Indies cricket as captain but we fell to a 2–0 series defeat – the first time Bangladesh had ever won a series away from home.

St Vincent and Grenada, where we played the two games, had two of the flattest pitches ever. I don't think I bowled badly on them and I certainly wasn't lacking passion and heart but my body wasn't strong enough. I was getting myself ready for the next first-class season and I wasn't expecting to get back into the West Indies side. My body just wasn't right. I wasn't injured – just not strong enough or fit enough to withstand two spells of 90-plus mph bowling.

It was an opportunity to showcase my talent but I took just two wickets in two Tests. Bangladesh played that series well but, come on, it was a West Indies A team against a Bangladesh first team. That's what I felt about the series. We just weren't ever strong enough in the first place.

I was left out the ODI squad that followed and Bangladesh took that series too. John Dyson was our coach back then – another Aussie – and he was a lot cooler than Bennett King. He spoke with me well and I enjoyed playing under him and his assistant coach, David Williams. But the double defeat to the Bangladeshis cost Dyson his job and he was sacked before the 2009 Champions Trophy in South Africa. Not exactly the preparation we needed.

I made the squad for the Champions Trophy but, with our

senior guys missing again, we didn't stand much hope. With David Williams now in sole charge, the group really bonded well. He was cool, just like Dyson, and a decent coach too. Being a former player – he played forty seven times for the West Indies, with some of the greatest ever in the 1990s – he had the respect of the players. He brought in Henderson Springer, the great Barbados coach, as his assistant too, which was great for me. He had good ideas to implement with the West Indies and I'm surprised he never got the main job. Maybe it'll happen one day.

But nothing could change the fact that we were at a huge disadvantage. How were we supposed to compete against the best in the world without our best players? West Indies cricket was struggling, big-time.

The disputes helped me play more games for the West Indies but I wasn't interested in that. I always want my country to field the best possible squad, even if I'm not part of it. I love the game and I love the West Indian people. I want them to feel good about where they live – not ashamed.

I played the one game in that tournament and, even though the figures may suggest otherwise, I didn't bowl badly. I went for 50 off my 6.3 overs against Pakistan without taking a wicket. I had it up around 93 mph but the Pakistanis just played it so well. It was our first loss of three as we went out at the group stages. Still, we didn't get embarrassed and, even now, I'm proud of how we did in those days of off-pitch turmoil.

The big boys were back for the tour of Australia after that and I didn't get picked. Typical. It capped off an emotionally distressing year. A girl I was in love with bailed on me because people were in her head. They were telling her that, after cricket, I would amount to nothing because I was from Haynesville and she was wealthier. What a load of crap. People have got to make their own decisions and she didn't.

On the cricket field, I'd had it tough too. I'd got back into the West Indies team – brilliant but I hadn't made the mark. As I partied on New Year's Eve in 2009, I couldn't have told you if I'd ever play for the West Indies again. I sat on the step of my mum's house, torn with emotion. I was twenty nine. I should have been at the peak of my powers but I needed to be better: a better player and a better person. I needed to handle people better, situations better, and not let anyone get in my head. I had to be a winner – and I had to look out for Tino.

Although I'd miss out on the World Cup because of my big gob, 2010 couldn't have started better. Courtney Browne was back, this time as the chairman of selectors for Barbados, and he told me it'd be a big year for me. I promised him I'd push hard for him and me and I was pumped. I was back under my big brother's wing, buzzing for the first game of the season against the Leeward Islands. Courtney had messaged me before, saying I was going to play, and he told me to get my head down, get some wickets and that I'd be back in the West Indies team in no time. It was just what I wanted to hear.

But then disaster struck: from being told I was playing to being bombed out the team. I was left on the bench after a management bust-up. Courtney gave the team to the manager but he changed it up and left me out. Courtney was fuming. I wasn't vexed but I felt people were trying to derail me. We drew that game and I was back in for the next one, in place of Nikolai Charles. A few weeks later, I'd taken five for forty one to bowl us to victory over the Windward Islands. Point proven.

I followed that up with the season's best figures of six for sixty five against Guyana and we overcame a strong Jamaica side in the final game of the season. Still, it wasn't enough. We ended up finishing second to the Jamaicans by three points, with the drawn first game costing us. I'm sure now that, if I'd have played that game, we'd have won. Anyhow, finishing the season with seventeen wickets at an average of twenty was a decent return.

A trip to Yorkshire followed and what an experience it was. I'm so grateful to Martyn Moxon for giving me the chance at the biggest English county ever and I loved every second of it. Injury forced me home early but my time at Headingley changed my life and my cricket career. I had a spring in my step again.

In 2012 we won four games in a row to top our group in the Caribbean T20 competition, during which time Fidel and I must have been bowling at 100 mph. We played a day-night game against Sussex in front of 23,000 screaming fans at the Kensington Oval and us two just ran through them. I took three of the top four and Fidel cleaned up the tail as we skittled them out for eighty nine. A good four-day season followed, where I took 17 wickets at 20.64 as we finished as runners-up. The West Indies selectors couldn't ignore me anymore.

This time I wouldn't be spouting my mouth off.

I sat and watched the five-match ODI series against Australia, in which we did really well to draw 2-2. Our bowling attack was made up of Kemar Roach, Dwayne Bravo, Sunil Narine, Darren Sammy and Andre Russell, while Kieron Pollard and Marlon Samuels got through some overs too. I hadn't played but being back in the fold, of a full-strength West Indies side, not a weakened one, was just so refreshing.

I bowled serious heat in the nets, just like I'd done for Barbados. Ottis Gibson, our coach, knew it but I had to sit and be patient. I knew my time would come if I kept doing the right things. It was hard being so close and not playing but I can honestly tell you now I never gave up hope of playing for the West Indies. Even now, I haven't. You're only ever a few performances away from getting back in the team.

I initially didn't get picked in the Test team for the tour of England that followed, although I suspected I'd get called in for the one-dayers. By that point, my big brother Courtney had gone from being a Barbados selector to a West Indies selector so, when Shannon Gabriel went down injured in the first Test, I had my chance.

Test cricket is just my thing. I love it – love the battles, love the fights. When I rocked up to Trent Bridge for the second Test and didn't get picked, I was disappointed. I was desperate to have another go at the English but, looking back, with jet lag following a long flight, it was hardly a surprise.

I was to get my chance in the third Test though and I had that feeling that things were so much different now. Where before it seemed to be all about me, now it wasn't. I was thirty one, I wasn't being billed as the next Malcolm Marshall and everyone knew all about me. This time the pressure was all on Sunil Narine, the mystery spinner who tweaked Kolkata Knight Riders to the IPL with all his trickery. I'd made my debut nine years earlier. I was there to enjoy myself.

And I did. I smashed it everywhere that memorable fourth day – and I loved every second of it. Ottis Gibson knew I could bat and asked me to put on 25 runs for the final wicked… 143 runs later, 95 of which were mine, I was out. Freddie Flintoff tweeted after the innings: 'Noooooooooo Tino! He went for the windows to reach his 100! Well played sir, great entertainment take a bow.' [sic] I wasn't worried about missing the 100. I was just delighted to be back.

Rain decimated that match but I will never forget how I felt when we got on the field to bowl. I walked down to fine-leg and the hairs on the back of my neck stood up. I was so glad God had given me the opportunity to play for the West Indies again. I cherished it even more now I was in my thirties than I had when I was twenty one. I was so grateful, I felt so proud and I was so lucky.

That innings changed my life. It helped me play Test cricket for two years, it helped me earn more money to finish the building of my home and earn more money to support my two wonderful children.

During that time, I played ten more Tests for my country and enjoyed cricket more than I'd done at any other time of my career.

Ottis Gibson and Richie Richardson, the team manager, handled me so well in those years and they were an absolute pleasure to play for. It was a much better management team than I'd ever experienced. Every time I took to the field, I felt Gibbo believed in me and I knew my role in the team: to bowl quick, word hard and listen to Darren Sammy. He, too, was great. When I bowled a bad ball, he'd continue to inspire me.

The energy was completely different with Darren in charge. He may not have been as talented as other captains but he gave players the energy to believe in themselves. The camp then was more mature than before too. Conversations were more grown-up. Guys were talking about buying sports cars in the early days and how they'd spend the money. Now chats would be about attaining property and about families and the kids.

We won our next three series after losing to England – winning six Tests in a row in the process. We beat New Zealand, got revenge on Bangladesh over there before Shane Shillingford spun us past Zimbabwe by the same 2–0 scoreline.

The wins over Bangladesh were particularly satisfying. I'd never played over there before and I found the pitches were particularly docile. Still, I took five for twenty four to bowl us to victory in the first Test and I followed that with six for forty in the second. Taking back-to-back five-fors in the sub-continent is something I'm so, so proud of. The second Test was particularly satisfying: I bowled with a hamstring pull and had to have three injections to keep me steaming in. That's how strong-minded I was. I'd have done anything – and still would do anything – for my country. That was the biggest achievement of my career.

During that time, we had mixed fortunes in one-day cricket. We were crushed 5–0 by Australia but, for me personally, in the two games I played, it was a decent series. I bowled some of the fastest stuff of my international career and got the speed-gun up to 96 mph at the MCG. I got Shane Watson out off the first ball of the game and then I bounced out Aaron Finch. These two were real aggressive batsmen but I had beaten them for pace in their own backyard. To play that game in front of 40,000 people at the MCG was magical and Bill Lawry, in the commentary box, was bigging me up as one of the quickest bowlers right now in the world. That meant so much.

I made my T20 international debut against Australia after that and I had the Australian crowd with me. Before the game, I was interviewed under the premise that I was the world's quickest bowler. I joked that I'd try to bowl at 100 mph and the fans were with me. They were all going 'woooooah' as I bowled and the speed would come up on the big screen and they'd urge me to bowl with more pace. It was great fun. I'd been to Australia under Bennett King and I was given no game-time. I'd just partied and had sex. Now, seven years later, I was back as one of the fastest bowlers in the world. It showed that, if I was managed properly, I had the ability.

I also ramped up the pace at Eden Gardens in Kolkata, in January 2014, against the Kiwis. I managed to keep Brendon McCullum quiet before he got down and ramped me for six over his head. It was one of the most astonishing shots I've ever seen. He'd done the same off Shaun Tait – that man has balls. I'd nicked McCullum off a couple of times before but, for him to do that, well played. I told him I'd knock his head off after and he missed the next one.

I love watching Brendon, who I rank as one of the modern legends of the game. He's one of the most aggressive and swashbuckling players of my era. He plays in a similar way in all three formats – yet he's a little more subtle in the Test game. He's just not afraid of anyone and he showed me just that.

But, if McCullum is a great, Mr Sachin Tendulkar is something else...

CHAPTER FIFTEEN

INCREDIBLE INDIA

'Tino sucks, Tino sucks, Tino sucks.'

It's 14 November 2013. I'm steaming in with all my might at the Wankhede Stadium in Mumbai. The ground's capacity is 30,000, so they say. But that's some way off. Try 40,000. Someone could have told me there were 120,000 spectators in the place and I would have believed them. People are sat in the aisles, or crammed up and down the stairs. And they are yelling, yelling and yelling even more.

'Tino sucks, Tino sucks, Tino sucks.' Louder, louder and louder, the noise grows.

They hate me, absolutely hate me. At the crease stands Sachin Tendulkar: a demi-god. He's carried the hopes of a cricket-mad nation upon the shoulders of his 5-ft, 5-in frame for twenty four years. It's his Test match number 200 – and this is his last hurrah. The last hurrah of one of the most incredible sporting careers ever. And he's playing in Mumbai, his backyard. He's the hometown hero, in his farewell Test, desperately chasing another century. He's scored 100 in international cricket and he's busting a gut for number 101.

There are Bollywood stars watching alongside Sachin's old team-mates and old enemies. Rahul Dravid, Ravi Shastri and VVS Laxman are all here. Sachin's mum, Rajni, is shown on the big screen being wheeled into the stadium. She has never, ever come to see her superstar son play at the Wankhede until now. Sachin's wife Anjali, daughter Sara and son Arjun are watching on. This is massive. Everyone is here. The stadium is one of the nicest I've ever been to around the world – but I'm the villain. I've got the Little Master starting to look uncomfortable – and they hate it.

Sachin's forty years old and I think I've got a chance. I'm bowling quick – real quick – and I figure I might be able to beat him for pace. This is the second Test of our two-Test series and I'm sure I had him LBW in the first. Absolutely sure he was out when I rapped him on the pads in Kolkata – but no. The legend survived that time. This time could be different.

Tendulkar is thirty eight not out overnight, going into day two and Sachin Fever has taken over India. We were skittled out for 122 in the first innings and India's reply had started well. Their fans are queuing desperately outside the ground to get a sight of their idol. Inside the ground, the boy from the small village of Richmond Gap has been given the first over.

I steam in, trying to hit the pitch hard; trying to crank it up. I'd hit Sachin on his pad in the last game and I wanted to do the same again. Despite his age, and his ageing eyes, he was still class personified. He was still getting his bat down really straight: the picture perfect technique. This was a battle. This was Test cricket. This was a legend at work.

But I think I've got a chance. I want to bowl short at him, then push it a bit fuller and wider and try to nick him off. Beating him for pace remains my best option. The fourth ball I bowl to the great man I send down short of a length at 90 mph. Tendulkar opens the face to flash and misses. It flies into Denesh Ramdin's gloves.

I hear a sound and go up hard. The rest of the slip cordon follows. Howzat. Howzat. Howzat. I was about to spoil the day of everyone in India. I'm pleading with umpire Richard Kettleborough – absolutely pleading. 'Give it out, give it out, give it out.' Put up that finger. But no. The legend lives on.

As Kettleborough shakes his head, the nation breathes a sigh of relief. Their man is safe, for now. I've got a short leg, two slips and a gully. I follow it up with a short ball and Sachin ducks. I'm giving it everything, absolutely everything. Sachin nods his head, as if to say, 'That's well bowled.' I smile, he smiles. The crowd greet it with a big 'oooh'. It's the most exciting spell I've ever bowled in my life.

I have made him uncomfortable and I plead with him to hook. I demonstrate with my hands and Sachin smiles again. In the first Test, I felt I'd beaten him for pace a bit and I could sense the greatness of the man was easing down. He may have been able to face Darren Sammy and the slower guys all day long but I don't think he liked the express pace. He might not like me right now and neither do his fans. People start to yell at me again. They're angry; livid. The Wankede Stadium is fuming. They see me gesticulate a hook shot and think I've sledged their god. So they get after me. 'Tino sucks, Tino sucks, Tino sucks...' Then boos. I'm the real-life pantomime villain.

If they thought I'd sledged, they were wrong. OK, it wouldn't have been out of character for me because people know I'm not shy of a word, but it would have been massively out of place. Here was one of the greatest sportsmen – let alone batsmen or cricketers – of his generation, in his last ever game, on his home ground. I respected that so much.

We'd given Sachin a guard of honour on day one. On day two, I said six words to him as he walked out on to the field: 'Good luck, legend. Now we dance.' He knew what I meant. He knew it was a battle and he knew I was going to go hard at him.

In the past, I had sledged Brian Lara but I was a kid back then. I was a rookie who had a wild side. That day, I had the backing of the Barbados boys too, in a domestic match. I regret that I went after him – I really do – and I learned from it. Never sledge a legend. Leave Lara alone, leave Sangakkarra alone, leave KP alone and leave Tendulkar alone. Now I was a slightly wiser thirty-two-year-old. I wasn't going to give it the verbals with Sachin.

But the crowd are still chanting. 'Tino sucks, Tino sucks, Tino sucks,' continues to fill the stands. I hear it and put my hands in the prayer position: the *namaste*. Instantly, the shouting stops and the jeers have turned to shrieks of 'yeaaaaah'. I have earned their forgiveness. Tendulkar had 1.2 billion people on his side. There are less than 40 million in the Caribbean but this is man versus man – and it's so riveting.

The next over and I'm bending my back, hurtling it down above 90 mph now. I bowl a good one, which he defends, but he doesn't look confident. The bat turns in his hand. I take heart. I go again, giving it everything. It's shorter this time and Tendulkar tries to ramp me over the keeper and misses. It wasn't a convincing shot and the crowd know it. I'm holding my own and loving it – loving every second of it. There are no nerves or sweaty palms. I've been real nervous twice: my first ball for Barbados and my first delivery in Test cricket. Now I just want to show I can mix it with the best. I have belief in my ability.

I felt on top but you can't keep a genius down for long. The crowd's 'Tino sucks' chant has changed to their more supportive one of, 'Sachin, Sachin, Sachin.' And he gives them what they want. The Little Master follows his wafty ramp with a straight drive. An effortless, glorious push that brings him to fifty – his sixty eighth in Test cricket. I slump to my knees as I try to stop it but it arrows past me to my right and goes whistling to the fence. He'd hit a couple of fours off Shane Shillingford that morning but this was his first off me: all timing, using all the pace.

The crowd erupts. Flags are waving and the decibel level goes up another notch. Sachin salutes them. I drag myself off my knees and go back to my mark, passing Sachin on the way. 'Shot, legend,' I say, and I pat him on the back. 'Thank you,' he replies and he pats me back. He's not belittling me; he's just being awesome. I am trying to take his head off but I love this bloke.

I round the over off with a short ball and the crowd respond with another 'ooooh'. They don't like it. Another bouncer follows in the next over. Another Sachin ramp. Another miss. I can sense the anxiety in the stands. The short balls are working. He's not getting hold of me. He said long after the game that he missed a couple of four balls off me with those ramps. I think I was beating him for pace.

I know I have one over left before Sammy removes me from the attack. Our coach, Ottis Gibson, had spelled it out before the game. It was hot, the pitch was absolutely flat and he wanted hostile, short, sharp bursts. So I had six balls to get him. One big push. I still fancy nicking him off but, when I try, Sachin responds with a beautiful back-foot cover drive for four. I send down a few more short ones: he ducks one, another hits his handle and the next he plays down and it hits short leg on the foot. I thought it was going to hand but it was a sharp chance: a real toughie.

Spell over. I'd bowled eighteen balls at Sachin. I'd had him hopping, I'd beaten the bat, appealed hard for a caught behind and ensured that he knew he was in a battle. I might have got him but the cricketing gods were shining on the cricketing god. For that whole spell, I was bowling at him and admiring him at the same time. I told Tamani I was going to get Sachin out for his thirteenth-birthday present. Unfortunately, it didn't happen. At least I got him a jersey, which is framed in his bedroom. He can, at least, be proud of that.

In fact, Tamani was very nearly called Sachin. I loved him that much. I wanted to name my son either Sachin or Makhaya, after my favourite bowler. I ended up with Tamani, but he very nearly ended up being named Sachin Best.

I wanted to get Sachin – the real one, not the close-to-being-named one – out or keep him quiet. OK, I hadn't got him but I had made his life difficult. And I had got his respect. Something I always have in the back of my mind is that I never want to be embarrassed. I hadn't been here. Sachin said in his book that Tino came at him really hard. To even get a mention in the great man's book is massive for me. I feel so honoured by that.

Five overs after my spell was ended, Sachin was gone. There'd be no final-century goodbye. Narsingh Deonarine has a knack for taking big wickets and there's none bigger than SR Tendulkar. He bowled a flat one outside off stump and Tendulkar could only edge it to Darren Sammy, with his big bucket hands, at first slip. Narsingh is one of those clever little off-spinners who broke partnerships. He was always capable enough for the big stage. As we celebrated, silence swept over the Wankede. After looking like he was having it easy, the legend had gone for seventy four.

The entire West Indies team and staff were so honoured to be playing Sachin that Test but, let's be clear, we were striving hard to get him. There was no room for sentiment – even if this man was cricketing royalty; the highest echelon of sporting greatness. As Sachin made his way off, I ran in to shake his hand once more. I had so much respect for him that I had to show it. This would be his last Test innings – his 329th – and he was leaving the field having scored 15,921 runs at an average of 53.78. There were 51 centuries among there, added to 49 in ODI cricket and another 18,426 runs. Wow.

Sammy's catch was a real good one and the crowd didn't like it. So it went from 'Tino sucks' one minute to 'Sammy sucks' the next. At least some of the attention was off me. Stopping Sachin getting a century was as good as it got in that Test. Cheteshwar Pujara made

113 and Rohit Sharma ended up on 111 not out as India reached 495 once Sachin had gone.

I did manage to get MS Dhoni out, caught by Sammy. It was the second time in two Tests I'd got him and, without bigging myself up too much, the one in Mumbai was a good nut, edged to slip. They were 365-5 at the time but I really enjoyed it and greeted it with a few punches of the air. He's a great player, Dhoni, especially in ODIs and T20. After Adam Gilchrist, I reckon he's the best wicket-keeper batsman ever. He's a fantastic human being too and he speaks very well.

But I was just never really intimidated by him on the field. I feel he can kill medium-pace and spin-bowling but it's different if you've got genuine pace. If you're aggressive at him, I think he struggles. Saying that, not many people have what I call genuine pace, so it's not like it's an easy weakness to exploit. I got him in ODI cricket before too so, in some ways, I like to think I had his card.

We needed 313 runs to make India bat again but we collapsed. Maybe that's just the story of West Indies cricket. I came in as a night-watchman after Kieran Powell went early but I lasted just seventeen balls. I was given out LBW to Pragyan Ojha but I wasn't happy. The English umpire, Nigel Llong, gave me and I felt it was a shit decision but it's the way it goes. I do feel bowlers get some rough calls when they're batting.

Another one came in 2004 when we were playing England at Sabina Park in the first Test. I was batting at eight and I felt in really good nick. I played a short-arm pull off Matthew Hoggard that was pure Gordon Greenidge style. The foot was in the air and it flew. Beautiful. Then Steve Harmison bowled a yorker at me that would have missed another three leg stumps. Except umpire Billy Bowden thought otherwise and he put his crooked figure up to give me out LBW. I couldn't believe it. It was a typical decision that bowlers often have to deal with. Billy saw me in the elevator later and apologised.

Fair play: he realised he'd got it wrong but it is annoying. I told him he'd never have given Trescothick out like that.

Back in Mumbai, Ramdin came in and made fifty three not out to stop it getting too embarrassing but victory was never in doubt. We had lost by an innings and 126 runs, meaning Sachin Tendulkar would never bat again in international cricket. I had a tear in my eye afterwards. He did a twenty-minute speech to a captivated crowd after and it was just so emotional. They had come in their droves to worship their hero. I didn't cry but I was close.

After a lap of the ground, the crowd went silent as Sachin walked out one last time to the Wankhede pitch. He bent down, kissed it, said a prayer and waved to everyone. Here was a god of cricket saying goodbye, twenty four years and one day after his debut. I recorded it all on my phone and still have it now. It was something I'll never forget, seeing possibly the greatest cricketer of our generation retire. I was honoured to play a small part in that occasion.

As a kid growing up in the 1990s and 2000s, Sachin Tendulkar and Brian Lara were always the greatest batsmen. I can't decide who was better but it was always between those two. Sachin was just the epiphany of the true professional cricketer. He ate properly, trained well and was a model to base yourself on. Any young cricketer would be so excited to be blessed with his presence.

And what was awesome was that he was always very chirpy with me. I met him in 2009 at the Champions Trophy in South Africa, where he gave me one of his jerseys. He came up to me and said, 'Tino Best, you are something else!'

I couldn't believe it. Oh my God. Sachin Tendulkar knows who I am. He explained how he remembered me running up to bowl at Freddie Flintoff in 2004 without a ball in my hand. Freddie had ducked and got angry, and I just laughed. Sachin told me he'd cried so hard watching that and how he appreciated the light-heartedness in the heat of battle. And, ever since, the legend had followed my career. At that moment, I felt like I'd achieved something. The greatest modern-day cricketer – maybe the greatest cricketer ever, bar Donald Bradman – had noticed me.

Even now, I remain so grateful that I had chance to play in Sachin's final Test match. After that, I was once in a hotel lobby with my very good friend Rohan Gavaskar, the son of Indian legend Sunil, and who I played with in the ICL. I got mobbed in that lobby. Forty or so people just ran at me wanting an autograph, a picture and, most importantly, they wanted to know what Tendulkar had told me after he'd made that fifty. 'What did he tell you? What did he say?' they'd ask. I was famous to them, just because I'd bowled at and touched Sachin. Imagine what it must have been like to be him.

It just shows how cricket is mental over there – absolutely huge. While on tour, often we couldn't leave our hotel rooms without security. Even going shopping could be hard. I'd go out looking to buy a pair of shoes and a T-shirt and it'd be an event. People who ran the stores would let you buy one, then tell you to take two more for free in exchange for a picture with you. The people are great. It's why I call it Incredible India.

Eight months after that final Test in Mumbai, I took on Sachin again. We were both playing in the Bicentenary Celebration match: a 50-over exhibition to mark the 200th anniversary of Lords. I was playing for the World XI and Sachin was captaining the MCC. I told him before that, 'Mate, I'm going to jog up and bowl good balls at you – no bouncers. I can't take it from the Indian fans anymore!' OK, I sent down a couple but he still managed to make forty four before being bowled by Muttiah Muralitharan.

Playing in India is always very intimidating. In the Caribbean the crowds are loud and there could be 25,000 there. In England and New Zealand you may have 40,000. Australia could be even bigger but India is just another level. Crowds of close to 100,000 people come in. It's just so riveting, so mind-boggling, and the energy is totally different from the Caribbean. The Caribbean can be loud but India is a notch up. You have to stay even more focused in the heat of battle. You have to be watching your captain constantly. Where does he want me in the field? Is he going to subtly move me? If you think you're going to hear him, no chance.

I already knew this long before Sachin's big swansong. In 2008 I spent a season playing in the controversial Indian Cricket League. The league wasn't recognised by the Board of Control for Cricket in India (BCCI) and, thus, the ICC didn't recognise it either. It was seen as a rebel league, with players threatened with being banned from playing for their countries if they took part.

At the time, I had little option. I didn't get an opportunity at the 2007 World Cup, despite feeling like I was bowling well. I was also left out the tour to England in 2007, so I felt enough was enough. I'd had a decent first-class season with Barbados and followed that up well in the Stanford T20 competition.

My agent said the ICL wanted me and were offering a really big three-year contract that would have earned me a hell of a lot of money. The West Indies hadn't picked me for close to two years and they hadn't given me a retainer contract, so I just had to go. They said the league would be sanctioned eventually and not to worry about it, so off I went to play in India and earn some big cash and to play against some greats. Marvin Atapattu, Damien Martyn, Jason Gillespie and co. were all there.

As much as I found the cash attractive, I'd done my research first. Wavell Hinds was off out there too and I had a good relationship with him from playing for the West Indies. He told me to never miss an opportunity to feed my family and filled me with positive thoughts. Merv Dillon and Brian Lara were also involved in it. I had made up my mind to follow.

I loved T20 cricket because it was just four overs of optimum pace. It was short, quick and easy on the body. I signed on for the Mumbai

Champs in March and walked into one of the sweetest environments I'd ever experienced as a player. The food, the hotels and the atmosphere were only bettered by Yorkshire. It was that good.

To play for Mumbai was a real honour. We had a decent team, led by Nathan Astle. He was cool and I never had any problems with him, and he was a decent captain – but we just didn't have a lot of batting support. We had Johan van der Wath and Michael Kasprowicz in our team too but I think what let us down was the lack of quality Indian players. If we'd had one or two with more quality, it could have been a turning point.

The training camps weren't going to kill you but they were good enough. We spent time running, sprinting and lifting weights. It was far from a military regime – and, thus, far from anything I'd done in the BDF Sports Programme – but we worked hard enough and the Australian trainers out there were really good.

We won two games, lost five and finished down in sixth of the eight-team table. I loved the challenge but the pitches didn't help me. They were just too slow and too docile; made for batting. I felt I didn't do too badly and I don't think I was embarrassed. But I went at over nine an over and took just a couple of wickets in my six appearances, so it could have gone better.

I got paid 75 per cent of my first year's money, as the financial crisis hit and lots of companies began to pull out. The fact the ICC didn't sanction it either didn't help. Nevertheless, I absolutely adored Kapil Dev and his people for trying to give us an opportunity with the league. Respect to him.

I knew I could be banned for playing for the West Indies but it didn't really weigh too much on my mind. If the worst happened, I'd be in the wilderness for two years but I still had plenty of time to come back. And, even still, Barbados couldn't stop me looking after my family, so I always had a career in domestic cricket, where I'd been successful, to fall back on.

Of course, the ICL wasn't without its problems. It's been well documented about a load of match-fixing claims that may or may not be true. One thing I do know, however, is that no one ever, ever approached me. I'm sure they know my passion and love for the game and would stay away. They know they can't try to influence me not to give 100 per cent.

But seeing that there are people who could have done it massively pisses me off. Cricket is the greatest sport and these people are disrespecting my game. I hate it. I never looked at a game and thought it might not quite be right but, if these claims are true, these people need punishing. It's sport – and you play to win.

The ICL paved the way for bigger things. Soon the IPL – the BCCI's own sanctioned rival league – was launched. It would go on to transform the way cricket was played, especially in T20. You can see how much cricketers progress by learning from the best. It's no surprise that the IPL has made Indian cricketers, who are being exposed to world-class players and world-class coaches every day, even stronger. I would still love to play in the IPL. If I never get the opportunity, clearly it wasn't to be, but it would be great to experience that.

CHAPTER SIXTEEN

THE END... AND THE FUTURE

After our promising run, Test defeats to India – where we said goodbye to Sachin – and New Zealand followed. I took eight wickets against the Kiwis, which wasn't a bad effort given that I didn't have much help. Jerome Taylor, Fidel Edwards and Kemar Roach were all missing, Shane Shillingford was being called for chucking with his action and Shannon Gabriel was just learning the ropes.

We lost the series 2–0 and it would be the last time I'd play Test cricket. Darren Sammy was replaced as captain by Denesh Ramdin, while Ottis Gibson was sacked the series after. I was dropped too and, as much as I understood it, it was tough to take. Darren and Ottis were just so good for West Indies cricket that it was devastating to see them go.

So, after fifty seven games for the West Indies, that was that. But I'll tell you now: I'll never ever, ever give up hope of playing for my country again. Even if it may be unlikely, I'll always have hope.

I sit back and look at life now and my love for cricket is still beyond comprehension. I'm still playing for Barbados and Lashings and I can honestly say I enjoy every minute of it. Cricket has taught me so many lessons and prepared me so well for life. I try never to be disappointed for too long because that's what cricket has taught me. It's given me some amazing highs, far outweighing the lows. I don't think I'll ever get hyped up for anything again like I did for cricket.

I enjoyed my path to the top so much and I'm happy with my career. I had an incredible journey but I'm under no illusions: I know I didn't set the world on fire. Still, I came through adversity to even play for Barbados. I wasn't good enough to make the age-group team and, if it wasn't for the South Africans noticing me, I could have ended up going to war instead. I could have died on a battlefield before thirty four, my age now. To even pull on that West Indies shirt once was a huge honour.

I boil so much of that down to the BDF Sports Programme. On 10 May 1998, when I started recruiting, my whole life changed. It's hard to even put into words my emotion on that pass-out parade, when I turned my head to my left and drilled past my mum in a slow march. To see the pride and happiness in her face puts butterflies in my stomach, even now. That's when it hit home that I could be a winner. Seeing Mum on that beautiful day really gave me energy to strive for the best: to play for the West Indies, make her proud and – unlike my father – to stay out of jail.

When I look back at my career, I know I was always hardworking, enthusiastic and a tremendous trainer who would consistently give it my all. That's what my coaches would tell you and that's what sums up Tino Best.

I may have been seen as hard work at times but I don't think any coaches would have bad things to say about me – apart from Bennett King. I was never hard to control. Wayne Daniel and Henderson Springer would pay testament to that.

As for my West Indies career, it was hot and cold. One thing's for sure: I never reached my true potential. I never had the proper backing. Take when I scored my ninety five, for example, against England in 2012. People will see a number eleven score ninety five and think it was a miracle – but it wasn't. I could have been an all-rounder. I could hit strongly, I liked fast bowling and I could play spin well. If I'd had the support system, I could have been a bowling all-rounder. Ottis Gibson's coach, Toby Radford, was so gutted that I didn't score a century. He'd been doing loads of batting drills with me, so it was no fluke that I scored some runs. I felt this innings was overdue.

I always felt I was a better batsman than the averages showed – and Toby agreed. He was rare in that he could see what I could do with a bat. That's one of the little things I look back on and wish was different. I have no regrets but I want to ensure no young cricketers miss out on fulfilling their potential. I don't want talent to go to waste.

That day was remarkable – but it hasn't been all smiles. When I first made the West Indies team, I had to deal with a horrible feeling of loneliness. There are so many different islands in the region and it seemed difficult for everyone to pull together as one team. No player should have to deal with that but it's been like it for so long. Unless the West Indies disbands and we play as individual islands, I don't know how things can really change.

I don't think the islands will ever go their separate ways but I can honestly say I'd love it to happen. Barbados versus Australia, imagine it now. I would love it so much if Barbados went alone and were left to make their way up the ICC rankings. I'm sure we'd do well. We've always had an awesome team and we produce the most international players per square kilometre in the world. We have a proven record of producing top-class cricketers. If anyone should break away, we should. We'd always play as a unit too. We'd encourage each other, be there for each other, take care of each other. The same can't be said for the West Indies.

Will it happen? No. I don't think so. So what we've got to do is get some women on the West Indies Cricket Board to make some big decisions. We need women executives, as a board of too many men is not a good thing. If the board is made up of ten members, surely three or four should be women. They calm things and help men make better decisions, just like my aunts, mother and grandmother did with me when I was growing up.

The insularity surrounding West Indies cricket has been around for years. When my uncle played, they had the same problems. The stories he told me were the same stories I experienced myself. There'd be guys off the field pulling hard for their particular island and it's not right. For too long the West Indies Cricket Board has been made up of people who are only interested in their own island and not the bigger picture. That must change.

Playing for the West Indies was both really good and really ugly. I've seen some tough things and the worst was the lack of support. At Barbados, you'll go through tough sessions but we'll all still be chirping away trying to inspire each other. With Yorkshire, it was the same. They'd give me so much support. I love that so much but it's so different with the West Indies. I've run in for the West Indies during Test matches and no one is clapping; no one is encouraging you to give it your all. This is Test cricket: why would you not be doing this?

If I was treated with the West Indies like I was with Barbados, I could have been a world beater. I've taken 210 first-class wickets at an average of 20 for them – that's incredible. I'm disappointed I never truly reached my potential as an international cricketer.

I look at Ottis Gibson and just wish he'd coached me the whole time, as I would have been a far better bowler. I've taken fifty seven wickets in my Test career, which lasted eleven years and twenty five Tests. If Gibbo was in charge throughout all that time, I reckon I'd have taken 250. I must have had the talent but it just goes to show I've never reached my full potential and that's down to the environment I was playing in.

I've always felt people didn't manage me the right way. If I had a run in the side, like Fidel did – he's played fifty five Test matches – I think I would have shone far more. We've both got similar Test bowling averages: mine is forty and his is thirty eight. I just felt like he got really good support, which I never did. In the Barbados environment, I used to play before him but, with the West Indies, he was ahead of me. I've got over 200 first-class wickets for Barbados and Fidel isn't close to me in that regard. It didn't make much sense.

When Sir Viv Richards was a selector, I felt he had faith in me. So in 2005, when he was cut, it was no surprise that I didn't get much of a look-in and everything went helter-skelter. If I'm being honest, no one with the West Indies believed in me after that until Gibson and Sammy and that was in the latter stages of my career. I played my best cricket under them because I had confidence that they backed me. I do sit and wonder what it could have been like if Ottis had been in the set-up earlier.

In the past, I had a reputation for being a bit wild and out of control, when really I think I just did things different to other people. To some, I was a breath of fresh air. Others loved me and, at the same time, others hated me. But, when I looked in the mirror, I knew I'd always given it my all on a cricket field.

US basketball player Kobe Bryant once summed up what he encountered in his career with the words, 'Love me or hate me, it's one or the other. Always has been. Hate my game, my swagger. Hate my fadeaway, my hunger. Hate that I'm a veteran. A champion. Hate that. Hate it with all your heart. And hate that I'm loved, for the exact same reasons.'

I read that and, you know what? He's right. People will love me for my passion, my hard work and my will-power. In the same breath, people will say I'm too exuberant and overzealous. Kobe couldn't have put it any better.

Some people are big fans of mine and others think I never fulfilled my potential but I will always know I gave it my all. What helps me the most is the knowledge that my peers respect me. I know legends of the game – Allan Donald, Makhaya Ntini and Brian Lara are three – respect me for the passion I showed every time I pulled on a shirt. Sachin Tendulkar wrote about me in his book. That is absolutely priceless.

As for the West Indies, we need to find a player who is a born leader; someone who can bring all the players together and put all the egos aside to work for the greater good of the Caribbean. Guys in the West Indies team are from such different backgrounds and they all have their different anthems: they're from Barbados, Antigua, Dominica, Grenada or Trinidad and so on. They've all got their own pledge so, when everyone's under one banner, there's no wonder it's so different. West Indies cricket is greater than all of us – it always will be – so the group always has to be the focus.

I do feel it's tough but a turnaround can happen. Lots of egos need to be dropped across the board: on and off the pitch. If a guy has a big IPL contract, he's not going to care about playing for the West Indies if there are problems behind the scenes. He'd just be thinking, 'Why am I putting up with the stress?'

The IPL is a massive tournament – an exhibition of sheer talent – but it's good and bad for West Indies cricket. It's good because it helps players improve as cricketers and it's a way to earn huge money, which makes them happy, yet it's bad because the big contracts mean players don't care as much about playing for the national team. That's why we need to find a leader to get everyone together.

We need someone to convince the best players to forget about the mega-money. We need to get players into a mindset that spending six weeks preparing for a big Test series, because the West Indies needs them, is more important than the pay cheque. We need to find a leader who brings back passion and focus, just like Clive Lloyd and Sir Viv Richards did.

We won't find this guy in a classroom and we're not going to groom him through high school – you have to be a born winner. You can't make these people: leadership skills are ingrained in you.

Would I give up $2 million to train for a Test series that the West Indies needed me for? Yes. I'd give it up because West Indies cricket is bigger than me. I've never played for money. I've played for adrenaline. No money can come close to the feeling of taking a five-wicket haul at Edgbaston, Lord's or the MCG. It's every player's choice to do what they want to do – but that's my motivation. When your country needs you, you have to answer their call.

West Indies cricket never seems to be easy. The strikes are so sad, yes, but sometimes I guess they are the last resort. I'd never strike, as I love cricket too much, but guys need taking care of and, at times, they haven't been. Here it comes back to needing a leader. A leader wouldn't let the players strike. A leader would make sure the players are comfortable and then sit down with them once the cricket's done to sort the problems.

When the West Indies pulled out of India in 2014, I wasn't a part of it but I was embarrassed by the whole thing. That's not how you deal with things. It was one of the most hurtful times I've had as a cricketer associated with the West Indies. I felt humiliated. A leader of a team wouldn't let Dwayne Bravo choose to go and play in the IPL and forget about Test cricket. And a leader wouldn't pick him again because then it becomes a Mickey Mouse show. Cricket is bigger than any one player.

I don't think the leader is born yet. If he has been, I haven't seen him. He needs to come up and through and transform the players. He needs to be the leader that Courtney Browne was. I always felt he should have captained the West Indies team. He's got that tenacity about him to be a leader of men.

I've never met a captain as awesome as Courtney. I've never met a leader with the willpower and encouragement that he brought. He'd get me at the top of my mark and have such simple conversations to get the best out of me. We'd walk out for a session and he'd get the group in a huddle and say the shortest of things. 'King and country, fellas. Here we go,' he'd say – and off we'd go. Those mannerisms, those little words and his persona inspired me so much. I've never held a team-mate in such high esteem as I have Courtney: a fantastic cricketer and a fantastic leader of men. We need a leader like Courtney.

I think this current West Indies crop – the likes of Jason Holder, Shai Hope, Jomel Warrican and Kraigg Brathwaite – are going to be a very good Test team in five years' time. They'll all be twenty seven, twenty eight and twenty nine and they'll be at the stage when they'll really blossom. If they come over and play county cricket in England, they'll get even better. That's vital to their development.

We have a lot of talent: we just need to get the best out of them. There's so much ability that just needs to be harnessed in the right way. Jason Holder is now in charge and I think he can become the captain the West Indies needs. What he has to do is make sure all the guys in the team believe in him. Any captaincy is hard work – it always is – but the West Indies job is even harder because of the insularity. He has to perform and, if he does, life will become far easier. He can't go out there, get no wickets for eighty, score twelve and expect guys to perform. It doesn't work like that. He needs to go and take three or four wickets, score sixty or seventy and lead from the front. Then the rest will follow.

I can't predict the future of the West Indies team but I do worry about the future of fast bowling. I absolutely love watching it but there seem to be fewer and fewer people who can bowl seriously quick. The 90 mph guys are a dying breed because you can't coach it. I enjoy watching Mitchell Starc and Josh Hazlewood, of Australia. Adam Milne, of New Zealand, is sharp but there's no one from England. The left-armer Tymal Mills, now at Sussex, is real quick but he's struggling with injuries.

And that's a common thing. People aren't built well enough to withstand the rigour of quick bowling. People say they shouldn't let kids lift weights but it's bollocks. Of course they can. The fourteen- and fifteen-year-olds should be lifting their own bodyweight, doing push-ups, sit-ups and deadlifts. Bowling is not a natural movement, so you have to strengthen your body to deal with it.

We in the Caribbean don't train our fast bowlers properly. Strength-and-conditioning work is started too late. Nowadays, bowlers are really working hard at the age of twenty three and twenty four but the attitudes need to change. Guys need to be stronger earlier. People say the heavy workload is the reason why guys aren't bowling quick consistently but I think it's because they're not strong enough. Until guys become stronger earlier – and I'm talking in the teens – fast bowlers will be rare. The only way we save it and harness it is by implementing proper strength and conditioning. When bowlers are strong, they graduate to real proper quick bowlers.

As for the future, I want to be a strength-and-conditioning bowling coach. I've been bowling at 90 mph for fifteen years now. People ask me how to bowl fast and I would love to pass on the keys to success – namely desire and attitude. I want to inspire fast bowlers in Barbados, the Caribbean and beyond. We've got to make players that just love bowling. We've got to build a desire to get them doing what they love. If we can give kids aged eight, nine and ten the chance to fall in love with the game, so they're shadow bowling in the shower or up the aisles of supermarkets, great.

Everyone says fast bowling is hard because the pitches are flat or your body hurts but you've got to get that out of players' heads.

Forget about the pitch: if you love bowling, you'll just do it. I want to inspire a generation of guys who love bowling quick; a generation of guys who'll never ever let people tell them they can't do something. I want to get guys working hard for themselves so every bit of talent is used.

The biggest disappointment in life is seeing someone become better than you at something because you don't do the hard work, even if you have more natural ability. As Henderson Springer always used to say, hard work will always beat talent when talent doesn't work hard. And I'll bring up one of my other coaches here too: Ottis Gibson. He used to say, 'Don't get bitter, get better.' I laughed at the quote at first when I heard it but he's right.

I have a 'five-minute rule' in life, where I let nothing vex me for more than five minutes. Whether it's to do with a girl, my mum, my son, my daughter, my finances or my cricket career, I'll give it five minutes – then that's that. I'll wait five minutes, drink a tall glass of water, then I'm good. People say I'm always happy and smiling – they say I'm the happiest man alive – and they're right. I don't let things bother me and I've got God with me.

God has done so much for me. My mum was never a big church-goer and my religious background comes through my grandmother, who went to The Sons of God Apostolic Spiritual Baptist Church for over fifty five years. It was run by a guy named Archbishop Granville Williams, in Ealing Grove, Christchurch, just ten minutes from my house. I was christened in that church and I love the place.

When the Archbishop passed away, I went to another church with my grandmother. I used to go every Friday and Sunday and I loved the place. I had such an awesome childhood, with the church helping me so much socially. I would have the greatest time, playing in the farmland with the horses and around the beach. It was just so good growing up there and always being very close to God. It's the reason why I'm so blessed now.

I don't try to force religion on my kids but Tamani prays a lot. My daughter, too, knows all about the Bible. My grandmother taught me that, if I could kneel before God, I could stand before any man, and she's right.

I've done a few things that God might not like in my time. He may not like the girls but I've always put God first. When I was a young man, I was a womaniser, but I'm not now. I was an athlete who got paid very well and had the chance to mingle with some stunning, gorgeous girls. I did just that and maybe God will hold it against me.

If he had to judge me, he may say, 'Well, Tino, you liked too many girls and that's the one thing I'm disappointed in you for.' But I love women, and I've never ever disrespected them. I will always respect people and always make sure those around me are comfortable and happy.

There'll never be any regrets with the playboy lifestyle I once lived, although I'll admit this: I'm sitting here now, writing this book and thinking about, one day, settling down. No one wants to be lonely, so I want to close in and find the girl who I want to get married to and spend the rest of my life with them.

There are so many people who've helped me on the journey I've been on. My godfathers, Denton Hoyte and Hazzary Prince, are two of them. They've been there every step of the way. My four aunts, my grandmother and, of course, my dear mother have all been so strong for me.

My mum never, ever gave up on me. At my primary school graduation, in April 1992, I played the clown role in a play as I came into it all too late. When I got home, Mum called me into her room and said she never, ever wanted to see me play a clown part again in any play or in life. She told me I was a winner – that I wasn't a clown – and those words have never left me to this day. Thank you, thank you, thank you. I love you with every bone in my body. I could not wish for better family and better people to have brought me up. I hope I've made you proud.

Timothy Boyce, Calvin Hope, OJ Simpson and the white-haired legend that is Conde Riley: without your help and guidance, I wouldn't be the human I am today. The same can be said for two of my biggest fans in the world: Richard and Chris King. Chris saw me in 2000 and said I'd run people off the wicket whenever Barbados gave me a chance. Well, Chris, I'd like to think you were right. Like Chris, Richard too was a loyal supporter through the good times and the bad.

As for my kids, who knows what the future will hold for them? Tamani says he wants to be a better cricketer than me and maybe he will be. But I always tell him that he doesn't have to be a cricketer to impress me. He could be a doctor, a lawyer, a garbage collector. He can do whatever he wants – but he must be an honest person. If he's honest, thankful and gracious to people around him, that's all I want. I want him to be an honest man, who isn't a criminal and who stays out of jail – unlike his grandfather. If both Tamani and young Thalia are good human beings, I'll have achieved what I want to achieve as a dad.

My very good friends Ryan Paul, Fernando Paul, Ryan Haynes, Aaron Barker and Paul Alleyn, who used to play cricket with me from dawn to dusk as kids, started it all off. Thank you, lads.

I always felt I was doing it for Rondell 'Crashy' Pollard and Davion Callendar, two friends who are sadly no longer with us. Davion was my neighbour, who grew up next to my grandmother's house, and we all played cricket together as kids. It broke my heart when he was paralysed at fourteen and he sadly died, aged thirty six, without having the chance to live his life to the full. It's such a sad story.

Vasbert Drakes worked so hard with me between 2009 and 2012, working every day to get me up to standard. What an incredible human being. I mightn't have even got that far without Sherwin Campbell and Clinton St Hill though. Had Sherwin not have asked Clinton if I could play the trial game all those years ago, and had Clinton not said yes, it would have been so different.

Moving on, the whole entire BDF Sports Programme should receive a big word of thanks. I miss those days so much and the place changed my life in so many positive ways. From my friends who stuck so closely together through recruiting, to the jealous people who turned against me, for different reasons, you all drove me on. If Sergeant Dave Sobers didn't come into work in a good mood the day he let me off to the trial match all those years ago, none of this would have been possible. You're a legend, Sarge.

My lawyer, Ralph Thorne, who is so inspirational to talk to on a daily basis, deserves a word. He went to the same primary school as my father and I know he will always be proud of anything I achieve.

My friends Steve Springer, Paul Skinner, and Paul Jenkins – and your lovely wife Candice – I will always love you guys for the love and support you've given me. To Miss Cicely Gray and my cricket mother, Ingrid, thanks for the help too.

My team-mates: Courtney, Floyd and the rest of the boys with Barbados and the West Indies. That includes Sulieman Benn, who has always been very close to my heart as another of my cricket brothers. He's one of those people who loves to cuss you but he will do it in the coolest way ever and it's just so funny. He is a hardcore guy. If I needed anyone to come and fight with me on the pitch, I'd want him by my side. I'd go down the trenches and go to war with Benny. He's one of the most awesome team-mates anyone could ask for. Thank you.

And the most important person of them all: Uncle Carlisle Best. He was my first hero, my rock, my demi-god... and my father. For me, he is the greatest cricketer who has ever lived. He's the greatest batsman, the greatest slip catcher, the most educated and the best talker. The way my uncle carried himself as a man was the most inspirational thing I could have had as a child. The first picture I put up in my house was of my uncle scoring a hundred against England. I'm so, so glad I've followed in his footsteps and played Test cricket for the West Indies.

Finally, my father. He's never been there for me, he's never watched me play and I've done it all without him. But you know what? I still love him. When he comes out of prison, I will try my best with him. As the great saying goes, you can choose your friends but not your family. I've never been embarrassed that my father is a drug addict who has been in and out of jail. Throughout that, I've been Tino la Bertram Best – the greatest. He was the one who brought me to this earth and gave me the name. The first copy of this book will go to him. Maybe he'll turn things round. Maybe.

TRIBUTES

PIERS MORGAN
British journalist, TV personality and cricket nut
0 Tests, 0 ODIs (Although he did face one over from Brett Lee and fractured his rib.)

Tino Best is a whirlwind of energy, talent, fun and fury.

That's what makes him so thrilling, whether he's steaming in to bowl 95 mph bouncers or trying to break windows with his bat…

Tino's the kind of guy I love to watch play cricket because he always gives it everything he's got, he's a ferocious competitor, and he never forgets it's a game and the crowd needs to be entertained.

He's also a great guy off the pitch, just as happy to laugh at himself as he is to laugh at others.

I recently recruited Tino to play in an annual game I host against my local village team. They've had all sorts of legends down there for this fixture, from Flintoff and Pietersen to Warne and Lara. But the moment I mentioned Tino's name, the local lads' eyes all lit up.

'Oh my God, that's going to be brilliant!' said one.

'He's going to break my ribs!' wailed another.

'Bet he's a right laugh!' said a third, chuckling.

'I'm scared...' admitted a fourth.

'We'd better get the windows protected,' said a fifth with a nod.

Everyone has an opinion about Tino Best and that's what makes him one of the most fascinating and engaging characters in the game.

DARREN SAMMY
Former West Indies captain
38 Tests, 46 ODIs

I had the pleasure of playing with and against Tino – aka Bobski – and one thing that was always present was the energy he brought with him on the field of play.

Playing against him was always a challenge as he just kept coming at you, whether it was verbally or with ball in hand. Playing with him, and being his captain for the West Indies and the St Lucia Zouks, I had to quickly understand Tino, the cricketer.

He's someone who is passionate, driven and very energetic on the field but also one who needed support, guidance and control. It is from those experiences on the field as his captain that Tino and I became great friends.

I will never forget that spell against Bangladesh where he ran through the Bangladesh batting line-up with a torn hamstring, picking up a five-for in the process. That was commitment to his country of the highest degree.

HENDERSON SPRINGER

Former West Indies assistant coach, Barbados coach and BDF Sports Programme coach

People in charge of the BDF Sports Programme said Tino wouldn't amount to anything much because he was mischievous and challenging. How wrong were they.

Tino, like many other youngsters, had his run-ins with authority. However, I am sure that this did not, in any way, sidetrack his vision for himself. He has achieved what many others dream about. He is not perfect, never was and probably never will be – but he's done something that many of us tried and failed at: realising his vision.

Tino is a great cricketer and a great human being. He's always been someone who has felt they've something to prove – and he has. In the Sports Programme, Tino was always the sharpest dressed in his military uniform. No one would drill as well as Tino.

Added to that, he is one of the hardest workers I've ever coached. He's always done a load of gym work and hardcore physical training to ensure he's in the best possible shape to succeed.

When the others might have been enjoying downtime and taking it easy, Tino would be doing things by himself. He'd run on his own and do gym work on his own – not because he's selfish but because he's iron-willed.

He'd always be practising for being the best: on and off the pitch. I remember Tino and another guy from the scheme – Lemar Wiggins – knocking around together. Wiggins would have a tape recorder and would play around, interviewing Tino as if he'd just won man-of-the-match in an imaginary game. He'd never have had a bad game – only good ones! Tino would go on about how well he'd done. It was all made up, of course, and very funny looking back.

Tino lost one of his great friends before his career had even started: Rondell 'Crashy' Pollard. When Tino's head was all over the place as a youngster, Rondell would try and bring him back to sanity. He really believed in Tino's ability.

His passing away, while on a football pitch, was so, so sad. Losing a guy like Rondell, at that age, could have ruined Tino. But he used it only as motivation and he soldiered on to great heights. Rondell would have been proud.

COURTNEY BROWNE
Barbados, West Indies
20 Tests, 46 ODIs

I first met Tino in 1991 when he was ten. He came into the Barbados dressing room with his Uncle Carlisle and you'd never miss him – both because of his love for cricket and his love for talking. He'd talk all day and the guys gave him gum to try to quiet him down – but it never really worked.

He was always very confident and passionate and knew he wanted to be a cricketer – and, through hard work, that's exactly what he achieved. There are not many men who worked harder than Tino.

I've kept to many fast bowlers in my time – Courtney Walsh, Curtly Ambrose and Malcolm Marshall, to name a few – but Tino was up there with the very quickest.

And the one thing he had which set him apart from his peers was his consistent pace over the years. He bowled quicker over a longer period of time – even now he still can get up to 90 mph on his day. He trained so hard physically and is so passionate about bowling fast that it has kept him going over the years. It was all down to his training.

Tino had a passion for bowling fast. As a captain, he always wanted me to bowl him. I knew that, so I starved him of the ball at times. It meant that, when he did get the chance, he'd bowl so quick and so fiery that he was capable of taking three or four wickets in five overs. We'd try and wind him up too, telling him he wasn't hitting the gloves hard enough or that he was a little bit slower than usual. That used to stoke him up even more.

He had pace going for him – and he had his mouth. In fact, his mouth was right up there with his pace! He had no problems giving it to batsmen and people across the region feared him. He'd be in their ears every ball but it wasn't just aggression. Tino was witty, quick and funny – and you could never, ever get the best of Tino Best.

There's one spell I will always remember that he bowled at a ground called Albion in Guyana. Anyone that played there knew it was one of the flattest pitches you will ever play on. Many a fast bowler ran from playing there. Except Tino. In that spell, he woke that pitch up. Fast bowlers feared it, hated it even, but Tino bowled so quick it came to life. There's not many fast bowlers I knew of or heard of that had done that at Albion.

What I loved, through all the highs and lows, was that the young boy who used to come into our changing room as a kid was exactly the same as a man playing for the West Indies. He never, ever changed. And behind the words and the pace was always a great father and a brilliant human being.

DICKIE BIRD
Yorkshire – 93 First Class games
23 years umpiring international cricket

I loved watching Tino charge in for the club I love: Yorkshire.

During his time at Headingley, I found him a very nice man, always with a smile on his face. He was one of those guys you could see really enjoyed what he did. He loved his cricket at Yorkshire – and I love watching players who enjoy what they're doing.

Tino will always be guaranteed a warm welcome whenever he returns to the club. People loved him – and I can't see why anyone wouldn't. He was that kind of guy.

As a bowler, he was real quick. To represent the West Indies, you're never going to be a mug. He fired it down so fast for us. He'll forever be a Yorkie.

ADAM HOLLIOAKE

Former England captain and Lashings team-mate

Four Tests, 34 ODIs

He may have been thirty three and it was twelve years after he made his Test debut and it's an exhibition match for Lashings CC. Has Tino slowed down? Not a chance.

I assure you, the man is rapid. He's bowling balls down to club players as fast as I've ever seen. I watched him real hard one game: tracking the ball from the moment it left his hand until it hit the wicket-keeper's gloves. It made me think my eyes were gone. I couldn't see it, it was that quick. Had I lost it? My eyes had deserted me, I was sure.

Except I've had them tested. They haven't gone – and he really is that fast. Other than Shoaib Akhtar and Brett Lee, I've never ever seen bowling like it. He's in that echelon. He's up there with the very quickest.

There are a few Surrey old boys playing for Lashings, a real successful bunch of former players. We talk about the good times, the trophies... and Tino. Imagine if we'd have had him as our overseas player? My aggressive captaincy, Tino's aggressive bowling. It'd have been so dangerous we would have killed people. It would have been similar to letting a kid playing with a power tool... someone's going to get hurt. All sorts could have happened!

Off the pitch, he has so much energy around the changing room. He's a ball of fun and excitement and is just so good to be around.

Tino's just a guy everyone wants in their team.

DAVID HOPPS
General editor of ESPNCricinfo

They shaved two inches off the Headingley square at the end of the 2009 season to try to liven up the pitches, but after experiencing it for the first time it shaved two years off Tino Best's life. It was fun to watch one of the most entertaining cricketers I have ever seen trying to cope. Flogging a dead horse would have been easier by comparison.

Tino had rolled up to Headingley as a short-term replacement for the Australian Ryan Harris, who was due at the end of May. It was quite a change of tone: a reliable and then largely unsung Australian professional replaced with a West Indies wild child.

He had arrived later than expected into the UK – a volcanic fast bowler held up, appropriately enough, by an erupting volcano which had deposited enough ash into the atmosphere to delay flights.

His previous cricket in England had been a disaster. Playing for Leek in the North Staffs South Cheshire League, he was released before he could answer charges of bowling deliberate beamers. 'I'm more humble now,' he said. 'You calm down as you get older.' Headingley tested that.

With his career at a low point, he needed an opportunity, however short-lived. He thanked Yorkshire, praised God and impressed with his fervour. But Leeds was not Barbados; the sun did not shine and the relaid square – although it eventually began to prove its worth – was not exactly gleaming with pace.

Tino spent his first day's cricket asking anxiously how much pace was in the wicket. Once he discovered the truth, he put on his headphones and patiently awaited Yorkshire's declaration. It came at 610-6, the eighth highest total in the county's history, when Jacques Rudolph had achieved a career-best 228 not out. God no longer seemed so benevolent.

He began at the Kirkstall Lane End, where Yorkshire's new £20 million pavilion stood like some space-age state school. After one over he asked to sprint uphill instead, with the decrepit old Football Stand this time serving as his backdrop. Neither did him any favours, but he persevered to finish with four for eighty six as he enlivened a dull draw.

He never bettered those figures and he could be wildly erratic. He managed only seventeen wickets in eight matches, but he never stopped trying to be the fastest bowler on earth. But his eternal optimism endeared him to a Yorkshire crowd that was not as judgmental as it might have been and preferred to look upon him fondly.

BARRY WILKINSON
Journalist

Tino Best is a misunderstood character.

He might come across to most people as arrogant and full of himself, but Tino is just an extremely confident individual who has built his life on being an honest cricketer.

All he ever wanted was to play cricket for the West Indies. I still remember Tino Best on his bicycle riding from the Kensington Oval to his grandmother's house and telling the whole of Richmond Gap that he just got a call to play for the West Indies.

May Day, 2003. Tino made his debut against Australia. I think he invited the whole of Barbados to see his first Test at the Kensington Oval. That day was a memorable one for me because it was a great pleasure to see Tino's dream come to life when he ran into bowl to Matthew Hayden.

If he had to be honest with himself, he would probably say his international career hasn't gone to plan, but from a regional perspective he remains one of the most successful bowlers to ever play for Barbados.

One of the most admirable things about Tino is that he has remained extremely fit throughout his career and I can only remember one occasion when he was unavailable to represent the island because of injury.

One major disappointment for me though is that Tino hasn't bowled in tandem with Fidel Edwards more often. I truly feel he would've progressed further with that kind of pace partner.

But say what you like about Tino la Bertram Best, you can never take away his confidence.

DEVON MALCOLM
England
40 Tests, 10 ODIs

We're playing for Lashings and out walks a club batsman. Tino has the ball in his hands, limbering up. Is there an off button? No. The man loves the game. He's just so professional and he's got so much pride that he's taking it as seriously as a Test match. He's not about to slack off.

So Tino puts his foot down, firing up all six cylinders. If you're willing to walk out there with a bat in hand to face him, he's not going to temper or turn it down. If you nick one through slips for four, the next one will be at your head. I told one of the club players that once and he thought I was joking. The next ball they were bounced.

Anyway, Tino is steaming in and he delivers one fast, full, sending the stump out the ground. He's bowled him. I can go on about how fast he's bowling or this and that – but I'll let the location of the bail do the talking. It's ended up going for six, sailing over the fence. I've never, ever seen that – and this is Tino bowling aged thirty four. He's still absolutely rapid.

I first met Tino in 1990 during my first England tour to the West Indies. He was an eight-year-old lad at the time and he just loved cricket: always hitting balls, throwing balls and wanting to bowl.

With his Uncle Carlisle in the West Indies side, Tino had access to all the England players and he made a beeline for me. He told me he loved fast bowling and said he'd play international cricket for the West Indies. He was so confident, with so much self-belief and confidence, from such a young age. Credit to him for backing up his words.

Tino is a great man around the dressing room: very confident, self-assured and not shy at all. On a one-to-one basis, he's a young man full of life, very amenable with a great sense of humour. He's the youngest of the Lashings players but he won't be afraid to give his opinion, joke, argue and talk about absolutely everything. Put simply, there's never a dull moment when Tino's around. He's the life and soul of our dressing room.

Tino has worked incredibly hard to do what he's done in cricket. He just trains so impressively and deserves everything he has achieved. He may be thirty four... but he could still be playing international cricket now.